TIN AND DIAMONDS
A fortune in the making

Something of the life of FRANCIS OATS,
Mining Engineer 1848 – 1918

And some thoughts about him by his Grand-daughter, Claire Leith

Frontispiece:

Francis Oats panning for tin in Swaziland with Francis Freathy
in the background while Giles looks on.

Published by The Trevithick Society
for the study of Cornish industrial archaeology and history

978-0-904040-74-6

Printed and bound in Cornwall by R. Booth Ltd.
Penryn, Cornwall Great Britain, TR10 9HH

Typesetting, layout and cover design by Peninsula Projects, Penzance, Cornwall

Moonshine and shadows and deadmen's talk,
Night is here again Punctual, black as my day
Behind the horizon,
Sponging its gossip like grains of sand
Soaking up the sea,
Holding hands with pain Moulding a death in the clay
And something more superior...........
And the threads are woven daily In and Out.

From the poem *Of Night and Day*
by Jenny Leith 1946 - 1970
Great-granddaughter of Francis Oats

This attempt at our grandfather's story is, with the permission
of his widow, dedicated to my brother

JOHN (JACK) FREATHY OATS MC

With love and in admiration for a brave soul.
Born Porthledden, St. Just 1914
Died Setubal, Portugal 1987

Francis Oats 1848-1918

CONTENTS

Poem by Jenny Leith and dedication to John Freathy Oats

INTRODUCTION AND ACKNOWLEDGEMENTS

Over the years I grew ever more interested in this grandfather who died four years before I was born; at the start mainly because my own mother had such an affection and respect for him and she told us interesting anecdotes about him - travel, family and so on. Later, my aunt Ethel Olds, when I questioned her, supplied me with earlier memories of Golant and Fowey and she, in her turn, had many reminiscences via her grandmother Oats, née Rundle, of her own life in this beautiful place.

I enjoyed coming down from Wales each year, sometimes twice, to go exploring, finding the farm where he was born and the mill where his mother grew up; then back to St. Just to look for graves in the old church yard, the house where he grew to adulthood and, of course, the mines where he began work.

My thanks are due to so many people I met on these travels. To Liz Luck, Golant, who introduced me to Mr. John Fenwick, the author of the splendid history 'The Parish of St. Sampson', although sadly he was to die soon after this meeting. There was a period too when my life was very unhappy and I was much encouraged by Sue Leith to continue working on this life - from the grave I was helped.

To Mr. Fred Harris, OBE, whom I first met in his office in Murdoch House, Redruth. I owe a debt; he was the first academic who told me not to give up. I also had great support in Kimberley, South Africa, from Dr. M. Buys, the Archivist of the De Beers Diamond Company, whom I met almost on a daily basis during my ten days in that city in 1990.

And then there is the late Mr. Leslie Douch, the archivist for the Courtney Library here in Truro, who managed to shuffle me and grandfather into the Journal of the Royal Institution of Cornwall in 1996.

Thank you gratefully,

ONE AND ALL.

CHAPTER 1
FAMILY ORIGINS

Forbears

Ludgvan seems to have been the original home of this Oats family of whom I am a member. In 1714 Martin Oats married; he had a son, James, but no mother's name is given. James was married in 1750 to Elizabeth Jennings and they had a large family, of whom Francis was born in 1767 and baptised at Towednack church, not far from St. Ives. It was not then as isolated as it appears today and many mines were working hereabouts and maybe James was employed on one of these. In due course this son, Francis, married Margaret Davey or Davy in 1794 in Lelant, at the parish church of St. Uny. It is through this Margaret that we are connected with the great scientist Humphrey Davy, or so it is rumoured, though I have not even managed to trace any of her family. She at least signed her name on the marriage certificate, but Francis put his mark and his occupation was a tinner.

He and Margaret had firstly a son, Francis born 1794, and then four daughters, of whom one died in childhood, and lastly a second son, Josiah, 17 years after Francis's birth.

If this first Francis could only make his mark it did not seem to stop his rise to a little prosperity for when he died he left various small properties and was called a yeoman in his will. His son Francis, some time before 1842, was tenant farmer at South Torfrey situated above the River Fowey in Golant (in the 1841 census he is an Oates!). His other son returned to Ludgvan to a small-holding there. His daughters all married.

Francis senior died in Trenwheal, only a little hamlet today, with two farms and a huge chapel, but here as in most places several mines worked and it must have been a busy place. He is buried in Ludgvan churchyard not far off from the porch. The slate headstone is in excellent condition with his name and dates and "I know that my Redeemer Liveth 1870".

Golant-by-Fowey

Many years ago when my children were growing up we rented a chalet at Sawmills, which lies between Golant and the old Bodmin Pill, where once goods were unloaded from the boats to be taken inland by horses. I knew that in Golant my grandfather had been born and that in Fowey lived cousins of my father whom we visited but just then life was too full of picnics, boating and swimming and not till many years later did I come on purpose to find Francis Oats' birthplace.

I stayed on the farm, Leyonne, and Mrs. Ruth Paul looked after me. I had been in correspondence with the National Trust at Lanhydrock about Cape Cornwall and

3

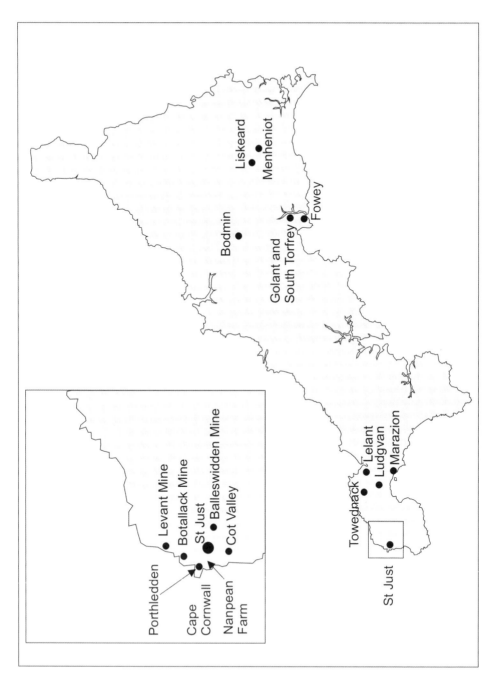

Map showing some of the Cornish localities.

4

family matters and now I was to meet Liz Luck who worked for the Trust and very happily it turned out that she lived across the road from South Torfrey. She took me to the Fisherman's Arms for lunch! A good beginning and she introduced me to Mr. John Fenwick whose fine "Story of Golant" was of constant help to me. Also of importance, she took me to meet Mr. and Mrs. White, the owners of South Torfrey. They most courteously allowed me to roam to and fro about the farm on more than one occasion.

What the second Francis Oats did until he came to farm here is unknown. Perhaps he was a tinner following in his father's footsteps and acquired enough money to set up farming, as so many miners did, as their youth went by. However it came about, here he was and up until 1842 he remained a bachelor.

Many of the buildings are, as he would remember them, built of stone and cob, and the orchard still grew sturdy old apple trees. Even the little house was hardly changed, a Victorian porch added, but the well beside the home remained. Up one of the tracks out of the farm yard, on the way to the higher fields, there was the gash made by the quarry once used to raise stone for buildings and hedges. Mr. White told me the area is still the same as back in the 1800s, 150 acres or 50 hectares.

He told me too, as I did not go to the outer reaches of the farm, that plenty of oak trees and some beech remained on their land above the river. It was easy to fill the yard with all the poultry, once on all farms, and dogs and cats and pigs, in the shed the cows at milking times and horses doing all the pulling of loads and work in the fields.

Golant is an unspoilt village beside and above the River Fowey, with the landing places and the inn nearby and climbing the lanes the cottages, and now a disused chapel and farms. On the crowning escarpment there is a church, with its little well and once a cell for St. Sampson, who stayed for a while there on his way out of Wales on his journey on to Brittany. None may know Cornwall fully who does not realise how such holy men tramped to and fro from Ireland and Wales and into Cornwall, some on to Brittany and even to Rome. No place too far and no seas too dangerous a thousand years and more ago.

It was in March 1842 that Francis Oats married, his bride Maria Rundle. She came from a family of millers and farmers across the Fowey, on one of its tributaries, the Lerryn. On the marriage certificate it states she was at the time residing in Liskeard. Here she had an elder sister with whom perhaps she resided and went out to work in the town. Her sister Ann, nine years her elder, was married to Edward Scantlebury. The house they lived in, 12 Carminow Terrace, is gone, buried under a bypass, but some of the row remains, numbers one to four I think. The good little museum in Liskeard have a postcard of the terrace when newly built and it was a Liskeard postman who warned me not to expect to see No. 12 and why not? I need to go again because in the will of Francis Oats senior it states he owned a share in Looe Mills, in the town, and mention of this will also explain why I know who lived at No. 12, for it was also owned by this Francis. It is my guess that his son Francis used to come up to Liskeard market and was entrusted by his father to collect rents! And at No. 12 he found Maria!

Well, to pass from my fantasy, back to March 1842 and proven facts. The wedding in March, 1842 at St. Sampson's, with the hope that the day was fair as a Cornish spring day should be, and after the ceremony all came happily down the lane to the farm. Maria's brother William signed the register and most likely gave her away, as her father had died the previous year. Surely good friends had spread a nice repast with, of course, plenty of cream and perhaps the local dish of ram pie.

South Torfrey Farm.

CENSUS 1851

South Torfrey, Golant-By-Fowey Farm (tenanted by Francis Oats 1830 -1856)

Francis Oats	Head, Farmer	56 years	
Maria	Wife	41 years	
Francis	Son	2 years	
Maria	Daughter	4 months	
Mick Rent Fury	Servant	26 yrs	born Ireland
Richard Harris	Servant	13 yrs	born Duloe, Cornwall
George Squire	Servant	13 yrs	St. Veep
Elizabeth Squire	Servant	20 yrs	St. Veep
John Willcock	Servant	16 yrs	Tywarddreath

Maria settled down with Francis and helped him in house and dairy in this snug little corner of Golant, the homestead sheltered by great elms and the lie of the land protecting them from the worst of the gales but the pattern of their lives changed in 1848 when in the December, was born a baby son, another Francis. What a great happiness to add to the Christmas celebrations as the baby was christened on Christ's birthday. Before two years had gone by came their daughter, Maria, to add to their joy and complete the family. So here in this cosy place the two babies grew into childhood.

Pleasuring in the Lerryn Valley and Nearby, Home to Our Forebears - Frethy and Rundle

It was my own aunt Ethel Olds who told me of the families hereabouts and how delicious the valleys were and the great trees. So on my second visit I stayed in a pub in Lostwithiel. I was dropped at the gates into Boconnoc Deer Park, May-time it was and very warm. I had previously written to the owner, Major Fortescue, who kindly gave his permission for me to look at Crickapit Mill on the estate. The mill had been revealed to me by some good sleuthing on my behalf by the Cornwall Record Office staff. For here it was the Rundles farmed and milled and Maria grew up.

It was in 1790 that the first John Rundle took on a lease of three lives and signed the papers with Lord Camelford's Steward. The lives were his own, his son John, then 18 years old and his daughter Rebecca, 16 years old. Later on, when I had read John's will, and with help too from the Record Office and also from a lady in USA, who was also researching her family, I discovered John and Jane Rundle in Menheniot, with three daughters first and then John and then Rebecca. Before the move to Crickapit, Jane was apparently dead and the elder daughters married. So here at the mill Rebecca kept house and John helped his father. Then, in 1794, this son married Elizabeth Frethy in Boconnoc Church and at the mill their large family grew up.

The first John died at the age of 89 and one of his granddaughters died young in 1827. Elizabeth was to have eight children over about a twenty year period. She came from Polpiece Farm, also on the Boconnoc Estate. Her parents were Giles and Anne Freethy [Haley]. Giles' brother Thomas farmed across at Hillside, another of Lord Camelford's properties.

It is through these two Frethy brothers that I recently found kindred in North Island, New Zealand. It was when I became a member of the Cornwall Family History Society and left notes on their files that relations in the USA and New Zealand wrote to me. I did know, through information from my Aunt Ethel Olds, that by way of Elizabeth's sister Jane we are related to the Cunninghams in Fowey. Jane married a Brokenshaw of Golant, a builder, and by and by they moved from Golant to Fowey. My father's cousin, Carrie Brokenshaw, married Jack Cunningham RN, who retired as a Rear Admiral. The family in Missouri are related through Maria Rundle's sister Rebecca.

To return to the mill and the day in May when all the air was scented with bluebells. The building in the 1990s was in fair condition with its mill wheel intact and even the name of the makers, Oatey and Martyn of Wadebridge, could be seen although

7

the wooden launder was falling into decay. The farmhouse stood on the slope across the track. I felt dismayed and lonely. I had not realised it would be so ruinous, with gaping paneless windows and doors hanging on one hinge. Later when I had found where the Lerryn flowed shallow and chattering across an old green track and I could paddle my tired feet and rest in the shade with the bank sides all bright with wild flowers, I could almost hear laughter and calls and comfort came stealing. After all, what were 200 years?

After my rest and dreams of relations hereabouts, I trudged up the lane to Broadoak (now Bradoc) church, set about with its graves more tree shrouded, I imagine, than in earlier times. Here I found the headstone to the second John Rundle who died in 1841. My holiday in Cornwall came to an end then and it was not till wild November days the following year that I could continue my searchings.

Mainly of William Rundle

The following year I went to stay with Doris Towler, who had been wife to John Cunningham, and so she was my relation by marriage and a long-suffering hostess she proved to be. The day she took me to search for William Rundle's mill was a saga in itself! It was a horrible day, she took her little car across the Bodinnick ferry whilst the wind and rain were doing their worst. The mill was at Peakswater and we found it quite soon. Nobody was at the mill-house but the mill had been turned into living accommodation. Here I luckily found the owner and she showed me the mill-wheel, still in position, but in need of repair. She and her family had just sold the place and she kindly gave me two photos. With the bad weather, I would not have any other record. She also told me folk further up Peaks Water could tell me more of the mill and its earlier tenants. So Doris motored down a not very decent path and then swooped down a steep dip to reach this house. The people were friendly but knew nothing. When we came to go, Doris's car could not grip on the fallen leaves from the sycamore. The man could not find a rope, so attached a huge chain to the car bumper. Doris revved the engine and roaring away behind the tractor we got halfway up the slope and then started to slide back, "Oh," groaned Doris in resignation, "the chain has wrenched the bumper off". I felt responsible and useless! However, it was the chain which had become undone and eventually we made the hill and the road and again Doris spoke "Well, that's that and now for the nearest pub," which turned out to be at Pelynt.

After lunch and alcohol we motored on towards Boconnoc, passing the farm I was sure was Polpiece, but I felt that as the day was so rotten and drawing in, best not to ask to stop! So we reached the church and I collected the key from an office and we inspected inside and looked for Rundle or Frethy graves without success.

It was high time for fireside and shutting out the November chill. Doris said quite mildly, "Next time you come to stay shall we leave the ancestors to themselves!"

The mill, Tresquite, I had managed to glean quite a lot about from old newspaper advertisements for sale or rent. I had also traced more of the Crickapit mill dwellers. The second John had given it up in about 1839-40. He, with his wife, came to live with William in the parish of Lansallos, which ran southwards to the sea. Here he died the following year and was buried in Braddock churchyard. The census of 1841

8

gives those living at the mill as William, his mother, his sister Maria and two servants. As we know, Maria was to marry the following year and I think perhaps she was only temporarily at the mill, possibly to help her mother care for her father. When I first found the records of her wedding I did not know her father had died and in my own imagination had pictured a smart gig taking them from the home Crickapit down the lanes and through Lostwithiel, spanking along behind a spirited cob!!

In the absence of any details about his elder brother John and with Maria and Francis for the time settled in Golant, William Rundle becomes important to me if only as an excuse to return as often as can be managed to this lovely part of Cornwall! In the census of 1851, he is still at the mill but by advertisements in local papers he is trying to lease it. In the same census I found intriguing reference to Charlotte Rundle, wife of a miller. She is 28 years old and has with her a 20 month old daughter, Rebecca. They were in the household that census night of one William Hosken, also in Lansallos parish. So who was this miller? In the census returns it stated that this baby was baptised at Braddock church in 1849, so I ordered a copy of this baptism and lo, who should be her father, but put as farmer at Cripstone, not miller, William Rundle!

Next discovery comes from the marriage certificate of William to Charlotte Polgreen Fowler born at Talland. The marriage was in 1843 and William is still miller of Tresquite and he is at the mill alone save for his loader in the 1851 census. His mother, then living at Cripstone died there in 1850.

In the 1861 census only the Scantleburys are mentioned at this farm; did the sale of the mill hang fire? Could William have journeyed betwixt mill and farm for a period? Why did his mother go to Cripstone to live sometime between 1841 and 1851? Whatever the outcome I shall have another happy opportunity for wandering their haunts once more and to visit Talland for the first time.

But now I need to re-cross the Fowey and look in on Francis Oats and his wife Maria with their children, Francis and Maria, all mentioned in the census of 1851 with five servants. But by the mid 50s the little Oats family had gone from South Torfrey farm, gone, lock, stock, and barrel!!

CHAPTER 2
THE FAMILY MOVES WEST

Settling down in St. Just-in-Penwith

What made the little Golant family come to this bustling, thriving, striving town on a windswept hill between moorland and the sea? There were good reasons, farming in the 1840s and 50s was in the doldrums. With the pending change of ownership of the Penrice estate, of which South Torfrey was a part, it was time to think of the future and Francis senior was no longer young. At first they did perhaps look in the local papers for another possible farm tenancy or in newspapers, which took in more of the county. It is a family hand-down that it was Maria's eye that lighted upon the advertisement of the bakery and grocers shop in St. Just. Much discussion must have gone on in the little farmhouse.

Another aspect high on the list of wants was a place to educate their children. In Golant they would need to go to Lostwithiel or to Fowey, in either case transport would have to be arranged, as it would be from any other farm. If they lived in the centre of St. Just there were schools close by, so maybe this was the deciding factor. So probably piling up their household belongings and themselves into a farm wagon kept for the purpose and with a suitable horse they set off for West Penwith.

The bakery was at No. 4 Church Street, a very old house, still a home today and with an unusual feature. On the gable ends are scrolls of stone and another house opposite has this noticeable architectural difference. Here were other old houses and across the road the fine granite church. Westwards the street ran into Market Square, then boasting a Market Hall. On the near corner stands the King's Arms and at the end of Fore Street the oldest inn, The Star. All about the Square, and radiating off it, there were fine buildings and beyond a second square, later called Bank Square, under construction with Bank House and shops. In Chapel Street was the Literary Institute, later the Lafrowda Club, given to the town by the Bolitho family. Beyond this, at the end of the street, was the huge strong Wesleyan chapel.

In St. Just and district, which was studded with mines, hardly a family would have been found which did not have at least one member a miner. Of those who were not, many were employed on the surface, including women and children. Farmers not only produced food but horses and mules and donkeys for work and transport and naturally the fodder to feed them. Fishermen supplied the staple diet. Today it is difficult to visualise the thousands employed then. My father, as a boy in the 1890s, remembers the Kenidjack Valley with its many workers and the pumps and works all up and down in this small area. People with even little money would invest in a mine and the talk was mostly of mining and how a certain mine was doing.

So into all this movement and business the Oats settled to hard work and almost from the start a school was found for Francis, and for Maria too, a little later. The school room was over a barn in Green Lane and can still be seen, although the outer steps have gone which gave access for the scholars. The schoolmaster was William Leatham. As a young miner at Wheal Edward he had lost an arm in an accident and went on to train to become a teacher. He was also a Methodist and a well-liked local preacher. Francis proved an apt pupil and, when older, became what was called a 'pupil teacher'. This meant that he might teach children younger than himself and also coach older pupils in need of help.

In 1861 his mother obtained a 'Certificate of Health' from Dr. Chenalls who had his surgery next door to No. 4. This simply said that her son, Francis Oats, was in good health. This was required before he moved to the Wesleyan school in Cape Cornwall Street and here too he became a pupil teacher. This was a rung towards training to become a full-time teacher. Perhaps his parents had hopes he would enter this profession.

No. 4 Church Street, seen from the church yard.

However this was not to be for when Francis was 14 years old he trudged off to work at Balleswidden Mine. Probably he went with others known to him, going down through the church fields and on up the hill to the mine. He would wear the traditional miner's duck jacket and trousers and a pair of stout boots.

Two stories filter through to us of how he was teased at first by the bal maids for his very short stature and also because he was known to be a 'scholar'. The second memory is that on certain days Francis used to walk into Penzance and, presumably, back again to St. Just after his shift in the mine was ended. He was attracted by lectures, presumably geology and possibly of mining, put on by the Royal Geological Society of Cornwall, founded in 1814.

William Leatham, St Just school master.

Francis would have worked on the surface at first and then gone underground with an older miner in charge of him. Jack Penhale, in his book 'The Mine Under The Sea', tells of the training of a boy-miner and the skills he needed to learn. First, from climbing the ladders to blasting the rock and much more. In Francis's early life two mines are paramount. Here he started on his mining life and learnt the ways and work of a miner. During the mid-1850s, Balleswidden Mine went through a poor period and it may be this that made Francis opt for a move to Botallack Mine on the coast. This was also a very rich old mine with workings out under the sea. Here he continued to work and soon made his mark, being made a mine captain by the time he was just 23 years old. This mine he was long to be associated with, both as a miner and a shareholder. The title 'Captain Frank' was a proud one and as such he was known amongst miners.

No. 4 Church Street was still home to him. His parents by now well-settled and well-known and friendships made. The bakery would have been busy and in those days people took their pies and pasties to the big ovens to be cooked at certain times. His mother Maria though was often homesick for the lovely rivers of the Lerryn and the Fowey and the quiet woods. She used to exclaim crossly of St. Just: "not a stick to scat a cat". These memories of hers came down through Ethel Olds, her granddaughter and my aunt. His father on his arrival also has a misty remembering, for he was said to mine over at Bartinney Downs Mine, to the south of St. Just. I think that at his age he would not have done so, more likely he made use of his horse and cart on the surface and only until the bake-house was up and thriving and, of course, his sister Maria was still at home, going to school and helping in the home.

Further Education

Francis Oats was born at a time when at last education was beginning to be offered to the working classes. He had the ability and the stamina to take advantage of these openings. In the St. Just Literary Club, later and better known as the Lafrowda Institute, lectures for adults had been established. Here were a library, committee room, a place where members might sit and read and a space for a caretakers lodgings.

In 1863 Francis became a member and the following year the Secretary; Mr. Boyns also proposed him for the post of Curator of the museum there, a position he was elected annually, except for 1872, until 1874 when he resigned prior to leaving the country. Lectures were held here by the Mining Association of Cornwall and Devon (MACD) founded in 1859, and here it was that he continued his education over the years from youth into manhood. His time must have been very fully occupied with these lectures and in reading a great deal both at the Club and at home in what free time he had from the mine.

Men of vision had been trying over many years to lay strong foundations for teaching the working men the theories of their trade and in this area men were predominantly miners. MACD classes were started quickly, the first two at Camborne and Pool and the third at St. Just. The first lecturer was Richard Pearce who had been a laboratory assistant in Truro for the Royal Institution. For us today it is very hard to realize what a breakthrough this was, with our free education into every known facet of known or unfolding fields of knowledge.

In 1863 the Miners Association adopted the Science and Art Department schemes so that students could obtain recognized certificates. Examiners were sent down annually to test the pupils and award the certificates. Here Francis came to the forefront doing very well in these examinations. In 1865 Richard Pearce left and was replaced by Dr. Clement Le Neve Foster. This was the man to whom Francis acknowledged a debt, saying in later life that it was through his help and teaching that he himself owed his success. This shows how great such encouragement at the start of a person's career can mean.

The year 1867 was quite a watershed for him. He did so well in this, year's

13

The Lafrowda Institute in Chapel Street, St Just.

examinations that many surprises came his way. This year Paris was holding an International Exhibition. In London, the Society of Art, long established for promoting the 'craft and artisan class' offered, through the Miners' Association, a gift of money to send a working miner to visit this exhibition. The way the Association decided to award this gift was to present it to the miner who did best in the May examinations.

At the Annual General Meeting in August Dr. Le Neve Foster had much praise for his pupil and Francis's results had won him a gold medal from the Department of Science and Art. He was awarded the £10 gift to use for the journey to the Paris Exhibition and, over and above all, he had won the right to attend lectures at the Royal School of Mines in London over a period of two years.

For Francis himself the journey too must have been a great thrill and then to be able to see so much of interest there. Of paramount importance would have been the exhibits of new mining equipment and inventions to further the ever-deepening of those mines. For instance, there were great new pumping engines being built for specific purposes and specific mines. This was a great time for inventions and Cornwall lagged behind no one. In the magazine of the MACD were reports of machinery, one recently written by his lecturer.

Back in Falmouth, the meeting of the MACD continued and still there was talk of this young miner. However, their deliberations on how funds could be raised to enable him to study in London for the two years came to naught. Dr. Le Neve Foster did his best to get some support but the sad fact was that the Society itself was badly off financially this year. The £150 for his board and lodgings seems pitifully little by today's standards, but it was a fair sum for those times. The best that was agreed on was to send a letter to Sir R Murchison at the Museum of Practical Geography to find out whether it would be possible, as Francis Oats was so young, to delay his tuition for a year or so. But nothing came of this.

So, when Francis returned to Cornwall, it was back to Botallack for him. Of course he was an 'all England gold-medallist' and had the praise of the Miners Association. But across the years there comes no whisper of the disappointment he must have assuredly felt.

However out of this same meeting in Falmouth came a very great concession that was to set Francis on yet another upward rung. It happened that the number of miners wanting to study had grown so much that there were not enough lecturers to teach them. The new, and what proved to be, excellent idea was that approved students should be allowed to teach the younger intake of miners the elementary basics of their craft, and all should be under the overall supervision of the lecturers.

Thus Francis became a teacher in his spare time, both at the Institute in St. Just and also over at Pendeen and reports indicate that he was an able and successful one. For the first year he was paid £5 and in 1869 it was £10.

The busy MACD meeting had even more to report. They had arranged for the students to go on an outing in the July just previous, to the mines at Chiverton up near St. Agnes on the north coast of the County. This had been a real success. Miners often had to travel long distances to and fro to their mines but had very little opportunity to get further afield. This new idea helped them in their quest for more and more education and stimulated their interest in another part of their County and meeting fellow workers in the lead and silver mines. There were descriptions of this day and of the mine workings by at least two miners, William Argall of Breage and Francis Oats of St. Just, printed in the Gazette of the Miners Association.

A Royal Day

A peep of light in at the window woke him. He lay quietly gazing at the low ceiling. After a while came a long stretch. He was a short stocky youth, 16 years old, this wakening Francis Oats,* mining at Balleswidden; working for his mining exams every free moment, and on certain evenings attending lectures across the Squares at Lafrowda Literary Club. What was he thinking about, as the dawn grew brighter, perhaps only pleasurable thoughts, such as today's holiday, and not having to trudge up the stony paths to the mine, down through the church fields and on to the turnpike road, this is the way he would have gone. Well, never mind, today he is not going there. He is, though, expecting to go to a mine, that very special old Botallack. No, not to work, nor to look for work either but to join the many others, all who could leave their jobs and home would be going there to greet their own Duke and Duchess. Prince and Princess of Wales they might be now, but the Sovereign's eldest son is born Duke of Cornwall. What a great honour, their coming to West Penwith and expecting to go down, down to the levels under the sea - bravo!

Suddenly the church clock strikes. The little room is filled with noise. Francis scrambles from bed and peers out across the street. Sunrise brightens the sky and pinks the little clouds sailing by – oh, I suppose the vergers will soon raise the flag on the tower. There is a short quietness as the notes die away.

Then from below a gentler tong-tong-tong sounds on his ear. Time is six? Seven? That is the old mahogany clock once owned by his grandfather over to Marazion.... it keeps time five minutes slow. The parlour is just below his bedroom and there the old clock has pride of place on the mantelpiece. His father has a great affection for it, and only he may wind it, once a week.

After the two clocks settle down, noises can be heard downstairs and steps outside his room. "Francis", a voice calls. It is his sister Maria's voice, "will you be down soon?" He answers in the affirmative and is soon dressed. His eyes are very blue, almost startlingly so, his hair is short and dark and like a thatch! He knows his mother is preparing breakfast and will need fresh water from the pump. His father has gone to early core at Bartinney Downs Mine. Not everyone can take this holiday, and the household needs the wages. Before he left he stoked the hearth fire, where the tay [sic] kettle hung, and soon had boiling water for tea. Maria, his mother would have been down early too, to make breakfast and pack up his meal. Now she was smiling at her son and daughter, as they busied themselves to help her and brushing back a wisp of hair that fell over her forehead. What did they eat for breakfast? Bread and dripping? Pilchards? Or a fry of bacon and taters? Well, something warm, and tea. By and by mother Maria opens the oven – it is already very hot in her kitchen – and out she slips two good pasties. Maria, her daughter, wraps each in a clean cloth. From the door her brother looks in, is she ready? She lays the pasties in a small wicker basket, wraps a short shawl about her, which she pins with a pretty brooch,

*Maybe Francis is called Frank - but as in the rest of the story I call him Francis, thought better to leave it so.

16

kisses her mother and away the two go. In the street they meet Amelia, who has been down the lane to fetch the milk. She will help her mistress, but has been promised time to go out and see the crowds, and perhaps the Prince and Princess pass by through St. Just.

The walk over the cliffs is as like and as unlike a walk there today can be. The like is the beauty of the sea and sky, the sea that is ever present around Cornwall, crashing against the rocks, or just a slow, powerful swell, even on a summer's day. Looking down, it is never quite a millpond, the sparkle is too fierce, the feeling of immensity and latent power is always there. In a fog, one feels there is nowhere else, just you and the hidden water-beast lapping below – then comes the moan of the fog horn, telling of danger, and help and men ever watchful, so that one is not quite alone. The sky, so often cloudy, so often full of rain on this western shore, has the spaciousness and clear beauty of the sea – one complements the other – and eyes here gaze often out to the horizon; small wonder there were always sailors and adventurers eager to leave the land and sail into the unknown.

Underfoot the turf was soft and springy as it is today but here the likeness alters and today we see sad ruins of an industry and gaze with admiration at the well-built and proportioned engine houses and stacks, so well-built that they take years to crumble, even on this wild coast. Francis and Maria walk by the living mines, where always a few workers even on such a day as today and on Sundays were needed to keep the mine in working order. Greetings and banter were exchanged as they went onward.

One who has not read some of the many good books available on the subject can have any conception of the enormous industry all about St. Just and through the greater part of Cornwall, at the heyday of the miners' prosperity. Mines and their works were everywhere. This was the industrial west, as busy and noisy and grimy as ever Sheffield was and then equally populous. Only a visitor with insight and a wish to know can turn these abandoned shafts and waste dumps clothed in brambles, and ruined buildings, back to work and people the valley with thousands of workers. It needs a huge leap.

I was going to mention the beautiful carpet of wild flowers we know here today, the streamside pretty with montbretia, water plants and cress. But the stream would have been heavy with mine waste – no flowers here then – perhaps on the cliff's edge there might have been thrift and campion. Only with thousands of mules, and later horses and wheeled traffic, and hand-barrows, tramping endlessly to and fro, and the waste rock being thrown out in higher and higher heaps, the flowers would have to be tough indeed to survive.

No more comparisons – let us go on with Francis and Maria, back in 1865. On each mine stood the count house (mine office), the very centre of the mine, where mine business was transacted. Here on setting day all miners, those just come up to grass, and the core about to go down (not sure about the third core – perhaps they also came) would gather, standing about expectantly before a certain large window or maybe about the foot of some steps. This day was not just pay-day but setting day when the pitches for the next five weeks were arranged. One miner might be able to take on a promising section, another less fortunate, having to return to a

17

The Crowns engine houses at Botallack Mine, circa 1900.

seemingly unproductive area. So there was hope and anxiety mixed in their minds as they waited the prompt opening of the window by their purser.

On this day in July, as Francis and Maria, joined by many comrades, converged on the last piece of open cliff land, a different count house met their gaze. Wonderful it was. All festooned with bright trappings and flags and, in front, a decorated arch. The Volunteer Artillery was also there, fine in their uniforms, waiting to be a guard of honour to the Royal pair!

The Royal pair, yes, the Prince and Princess of Wales, our own Duke and Duchess of Cornwall, soon would arrive to go underground. Oh the excitement! And what an honour for us! Earlier on this day they had left St. Michael's Mount with their host and hostess, the Lord and Lady St. Aubyn, rowed across to the quay below St. Mary's church at Penzance. In the bay the Royal Yacht *Osborne* rode at anchor. By the quayside the carriage is in readiness, four greys to draw it. The royal party only stop at the seaward end of the new roadway, whilst the Princess names it Alexandra Road! On through Newlyn and to St. Just all en fete for the royal couple and crowded with loyal sightseers. Perhaps Maria Oats had a signal from Amelia, her maid and, just in time, threw away her floury apron, and came to the corner of the Square, waving and cheering "all in glorious summer weather".

Francis and Maria would be one of this vast crowd dotted about over the mine and perched on rocky outcrops, almost to the cliff edge. Soon horses' hooves are heard, and distant cheering, and the royal party sweeps up to the count house. The

18

Volunteers present arms, and the band plays God Save the Queen and God Bless the Prince of Wales as the Prince and Princess enter the count house. There the Prince is offered an underground suit and the Princess a pair of boots.

Outside once more, the Princess and Lady St. Aubyn are drawn towards the gig by a donkey and shay. Princess Alexandra, this extremely beautiful woman, wore a white cloak and a straw boater, both trimmed with blue ribbon. Only two years earlier this very same gig had been the centre of a terrible tragedy – no one surviving to tell the whole tale. There was no sign of fear as the party disappeared down the dark shaft. Captain Rowe was in charge, with his hand on the safety brake, the gig glided off, the steel wire unwinding as it drew them down.

Everything goes well and a great cheer goes up when they return. The gig goes down three more times before the carriages carry all away from the mine; the crowd has had a happy time, and gradually disperses. No-one is in too great a hurry. It is a memorable day, and here too folk will find friends or relatives from other parishes and so enjoy the lovely sunshine and a rest from everyday chores. Francis and Maria set off for home joining with others going to the little grey town on the hill, and soon there is the flag of St. George fluttering from the church tower, its red and white showing brightly against the summer blue sky, pin-pointing the almost exact spot where their home is, if they needed such guidance.

Later in the day, Francis changes into rough clothes and boots and once more crosses the squares. He waits beside the Lafrowda Institute. Soon two other youngsters approach and with cheery greetings the three march off on their way down to the cove. They walk the footpath to Boswedden Farm over several stiles, the last one directly beside the little granite farmhouse. In the valley beyond lie Boswedden and Wheal Castle Mine and as they near the seashore, more mines St. Just United and Cape Cornwall with its new great stack rearing up on the summit of the headland. Just now mines are not foremost in their minds. Down in Priest's Cove, two men are busy fitting out a boat. These are two miners who share the boat with two others. Also, they are the fathers of Francis's two companions. The youths run down to the rocky cove, and soon it is a heave, a heave and a heave, and the boat slides over the gritty sand. One more hefty shove and it is in the water. All scramble aboard, one to the rudder, two to the oars and two will hoist the sails when needed. All are busy. The wind lifts them, the sea swells and sparkles. What will they catch for supper? Already one can see the fish cleaned, split and sizzling on Mother Maria's fire, ready to eat accompanied by good bread.

Young Francis Oats, you will always love this place and return and return, and sometimes maybe remember too the woods by the river where you were born but your life will be spent pioneering in a vast, wondrous land, scorched and dusty sometimes, and you will dream then of the green grass of Cornwall and the sea that is all about her.

At Botallack Mine

The history of this old mine has been recounted in Cyril Noall's book and I only wish everyone might read it. Such a saga of success and jubilation and then falling on bad times, only to struggle upwards again, not once but many times until finally in 1895, as no bidders came forward, the mine was closed and dismantled, in the same way as Balleswidden and most other mines throughout Cornwall, suffered the same fate. A knacked bal is a sad sight, like a deserted house, with all the inmates gone.

Botallack, like Balleswidden has an extra interest here. In the latter Francis Oats began to learn his mining skills, and at Botallack he put them to use and became responsible for the running of a part of the mine. We do not know when he left Balleswidden but there are records of him at Botallack, and even when he had departed to South Africa in 1874. He held shares in the old mine, and attended board meetings when he came over from South Africa, usually every 18 months or 2 years.

Changes 1870-1874

As "Captain Frank" will Francis Oats be known to Cornishmen and in the mining community. Only working miners in charge of certain sections of the mine or in charge of certain working processes of a mine may be so addressed and it is a proud title but St. Just and the mining areas are about to suffer. No longer is the town the prosperous place the Oats found but twenty years earlier. Malaysian tin found much more easily and more cheaply is about to flood the market and Cornwall fall from prominence. Knacked (closed) bals were everywhere and more and more miners were paid off. Prices of coal and transport kept rising. Great efforts were made to keep the mines open for they were the cornerstone of so much of the population. It was a losing battle. Men left for mines overseas in ever increasing numbers. Houses stood empty. Poverty and gloom made the mining town a sad place and doubtless Maria would sell much 'on tick' or wait to be paid till money came from overseas.

The census of 1871 shows Captain Frank's father still head of the household at 77 years of age but Maria the daughter is missing. By then she was married to Henry Olds, eldest son of John Olds and his wife, Elizabeth, née Peake. They lived in Carrallack Terrace when they were first married. He was a staunch Methodist. Later in life he farmed Letcha above the Cot Valley. He held a good many Levant shares and attended most count house meetings, where later he used to stand in for his brother-in-law, when he was absent in South Africa. Francis was to entrust him too with completing the purchase of a house in St. Just for his family to occupy but this is ahead of time.

Before the year 1871 was out, the head of the Church Street household was dead. He was buried in the 'new' church burial ground outside the main one at the parish Church. Neither today is used for burials. Maria remained at No. 4 Church Street, as far as we know, and had then a 16 year old girl, Mary Hocking, to help her.

The next big change was the wedding of Francis to Elizabeth Ann, sister to Henry. They were married in the parish church 'across the street' in August 1874. I hope they had a lovely peal of bells, as I did 70 years later. It is through these marriages into the same family of Olds that the Oats became related to so many folk in St. Just. Francis and Maria were not to be long together, for earlier he had applied and been accepted as a mining engineer by the Colonial Office and he was to go out to Griqualand West in South Africa shortly. In the first instance, as was usual, he would go alone.

CHAPTER 3
THERE AND BACK AGAIN

Exodus

Quiller Couch writing of his home town Fowey at this time said "The event of those days would be the arrival or departure of one of its two sailing brigs, bringing home, in lessening quantity, timber for mine props, carrying away, in gathering numbers, the Duchy's youth". The West Briton newspaper of November, 1877 reports; "The present depression has probably been felt more heavily in St. Just than anywhere else. At the last census it had a population of 9,000 souls but that this has very much decreased is shown by the fact that at the last poor rate assessment, no less than 280 houses were struck off the list as unoccupied."

So with many another, Francis set off on the long journey to South Africa. Special trains left Cornwall to take the crowds, mainly miners, to the embarkation ports. It is known that Francis Oats had two other St. Justers travelling at the same time. One was Jonathan Samson, related to the Tippet family. The stations on these days must have been packed, Penzance the start, Marazion, St. Erth, Hayle, Camborne and Redruth.

The goodbyes, the hopes and the heartbreak of a whole tight knit community focused there in those little stations. The platforms with the wives, children and other relatives, the men crowding the windows of the train. The guard raised his green flag, his whistle shrilled, the engine added its awful hiss of escaping steam and pounding and throbbing like the hearts of all present, the powerful monster drew its load away up through Cornwall. Once across Brunel's bridge over the Tamar, the foreign travel was begun and Francis Oats was on his way.

To a Far Country

Man's main task in life is to give birth to himself, to become what he potentially is. The most important produce of his efforts is his own personality.
From Man for Himself by Eric Fromm.

The steamers to Cape Town in South Africa in 1874 took about 30 days although the time decreased yearly. On docking, Francis Oats would have seen his luggage landed safely and probably taken a hansom cab up to the centre of the town, perhaps sharing with the two other St. Justers. Their first need would be to arrange some cheap lodging and find out the time next day for the train and the transport to Barkly West. The other two men were going to the diggings and time was their own as long as the money held out, but Francis had a definite post to go to. Jonathan Samson did not stay long in South Africa, he told folk at home he did not like the dust or the flies! He went, on return, to work on mines in the Newcastle area. Later in life, on a visit to St. Just when Porthledden was being built, he remarked perhaps it was a pity he

21

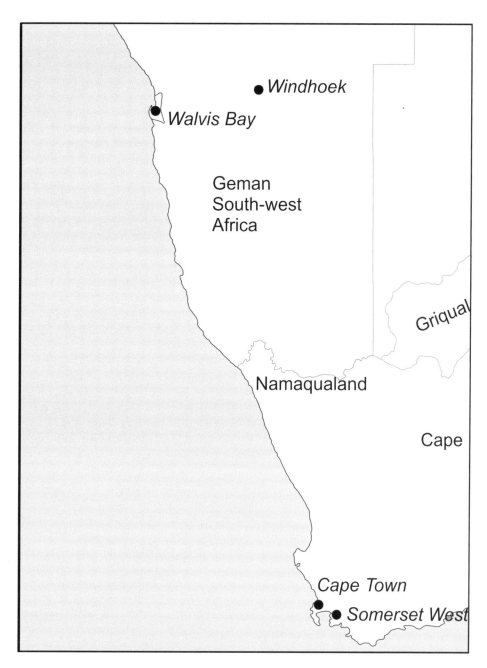

Map showing some of the South African locations, circa 1890.

Bechuanaland

Transvaal

South African
Republic

● *Pretoria*

● *Witwatersrand*

and West ● *Vryburg*

Barkly West Orange Free
State

Kimberley

● *Ladysmith*

Natal

Colony

East
Griqualand

Zululand

Mozambique

● *Port Elizabeth*

had not remained in South Africa!

At that time the railway only went about 60 miles northward, as far as Wellington. From there the remaining 600 miles had to be taken in some form of wheeled transport. In due course, after a jolting tiring tourney, Francis was deposited in Barkly West which recently by decree, had its name changed from Klipsdrift. This place had been the centre of the diggings which had now shifted across the river. Whoever was in charge of this now sleepy place, after reading Francis's introductory letter sent him on to Kimberley with a letter to either the Lieutenant Governor Southey or the Colonial Secretary, John Currey, suggesting that a place on the Mining Board be offered. This Board had only been recently created and was Currey's 'pet' project. By February, Francis was settled in his own office, if only the usual iron shack, and in a short time was busy about the four mines, meeting the diggers and finding out first-hand, the problems and dangers of their work.

As early as March he had prepared his report for the Colonial Office, which went first to the Lieutenant Governor of Cape Province, Sir Henry Barkly. I saw a copy of this report in the Afrikaner's Library in Kimberley. This library holds an immense amount of material about Kimberley and much about this time, including a copy of Crossman's official report to the Government (more later). This report I first saw in the Public Records Office at Kew, and, of course, they hold the official letters and reports to do with Griqualand West, the area where diamonds were discovered.

To understand both the place and the time one has to read fairly extensively. Between late 1874 and 1876 Francis Oats was plumped into a period of disturbance and excitement. There were boundary disputes and diamond thieving was rife, not to mention that there was a slump in the ordinary sale of the diamonds. The ever-increasing depth of the diggings brought danger, with falls of cliff and mud rushes. Southey the Governor had not long been in office and the Colonial Secretary had from the start upset the miners, treating them as inferiors and setting up this new Board on which they were very poorly represented. Southey's belief held that all were equal under the law and expected black men to be treated similarly to white men. Already all the latter wished was to keep the black man in subjugation, using them simply for labouring and as servants.

It is far too complicated to be treated by me, and certainly not in a short space. Francis as we know had never been a digger but had been a working miner so knew how independent they could be. However, he was here as an employee of the Colonial Office to write them a report on the four mines. He was competent and thorough in putting forward plans for improvements. He did these in constant conference with the diggers, with whom by his upbringing and instincts he was in sympathy. Indeed, I feel it was a tricky time for him, balanced between the miners and government authority.

In Kimberley when he arrived it was high summer and the place was stiflingly hot, dusty and full of flies. Dust storms were frequent; clouds whipped up from the diggings and the debris heaps, making for extreme discomfort. Tents could be torn down and shacks flattened. Later the winter months bitter winds and frost could be experienced. Wood for fires was scarce and expensive. Even in hot times the temperature fell quickly at nightfall. All diggers needed warm clothing and blankets which they brought up from the coast. Water was also scarce and sanitation of the rudest. Sickness was rife with dysentery, skin diseases and malaria, which was called 'camp sickness'.

Francis was to be based in Kimberley for the rest of his life. In 1875 he stood on the threshold of his career but only a crystal gazer could see what a fine place Kimberley would grow into and how prominent a person he would become.

One endearing characteristic of Kimberley people was their sense of fun. When there was a crisis they used to stage outward displays. Everyone enjoyed a picnic, taking wagons, perhaps to Alexanderfontein, where there were trees and the river. Cricket matches were arranged and horse racing was, early on, a great enthusiasm. Some went off fishing or hunting for relaxation. On the pending arrival of the new Governor and his lady, almost the whole town turned out to welcome them, placing them in a fine carriage with mettlesome horses for the last stage of their journey, offering speeches of welcome, a marvellous repast in a brand new canteen and rounding all off with fireworks in the evening. Sad that such a bright start should end so grimly.

Francis Oats can certainly have had few dull moments and to add to the excitement this was the year of the Black Flag Rebellion. At the first finds of diamonds the diggers made their own laws and had their own committee to enforce them.

Later, when the diamond finds seemed likely to continue, Britain annexed Griqualand West and sent three Commissioners up to the fields who thoroughly upset the diggers by taking over their authority. Resentment led to unrest. There were many problems but the Commissioners could not solve them and rioting began. Police were too few and eventually Sir Henry Barkly felt compelled to come up to the fields himself. He admitted it was wrong to try to govern them from the Cape. He told them he proposed to set up a Crown Colony, with its own Governor and its own Legislature, so they might arrange matters themselves. So the diggers cheered the Cape Governor and by and by, as we know, Robert Southey arrived. He also was unable to settle the disputes and his own views were very far from those of the miners.

Things boiled over. In August, 1874, the miners set up a Committee of their own and started, at first, secretly training armed bands and then openly. Their grievances were aired in a local paper and Southey promptly sent police to arrest the editor. The Governor began training Special Constables, some of them black men, and sent for troops in June, 1875. Again there were changes – Lord Caernarvon, Secretary for the Colonies, had Southey relieved of his post and Currey was also forced to retire.

The Colonial Office was "sending out a competent person to report on the mining community" and to "recommend further economies". So arrived in November 1875 His Excellency Major (later Sir) W. Owen Lanyon, appointed as Administrator for Kimberley. He got on with his duties, not sure if he had a rousing welcome and soon after his arrival another important figure took the stage. This was Colonel Crossman, the Royal Commissioner. He was to inquire into the financial state of the Colony, which devolved mainly into an investigation into the state of the mining industry, and in its train brought to his notice all the grievances long held by the diggers against the Government.

During December, 1875 to February, 1876, Colonel Crossman held courts of inquiry, sending his reports back to the Colonial Office in February and May, 1875. The whole report is of immense interest. Francis Oats had at least two interviews, and his own mining report is in part incorporated into the Crossman papers (these can be read in full in London and in Kimberley).

This is, I think, when I first found my grandfather, I mean to feel him and whatever follows afterwards in his life, and there are quite direct places I feel his presence, here my respect for him awakens. All rather personal, so forgive me. It is the fact that by his report he advocates the abolition of many Government posts in the interests of better government and of saving expenses for the Colony, his own post would be one to be axed. This seems very much in keeping with his character, that what is best for the mining interests must be carried out.

Two intriguing little items remain to this period in Francis Oats coming to Kimberley. Mention must be made of Cecil Rhodes already being a personage in Kimberley and with whom Francis Oats' own career was eventually involved. Here it is they first must have met and it was Rhodes who approached Oats to ask his advice about the size of pumps he needed to install in some of the mine workings. Rhodes was to be noted for his access to men who could be of use to him and also for quickly casting off those he no longer had a use for! From such small beginnings!

The other little personal matter refers to the meetings with Crossman, for before the second interview he had been granted, Francis wrote a letter to Colonel Crossman telling him he had a matter both private and personal to impart to him prior to the interview. And there one is left tantalised. Whatever could it have been about?

For Informing Myself

Go far, come near, you still must be the centre of your own small mystery"
Walter de la Mare

Francis Oats' post of Provincial Engineer, along with those of the Government Surveyors and Registrars and their Clerks, was abolished. How high were his hopes when he first came out, good wages and an influential position and in so short a time these dashed to the ground and the prospects for him in Africa seemed bleak. He had been in Kimberley long enough to know its community, to have been touched by its troubles, by its jealousies, and loyalties and to have seen its gaiety in the face of such problems. He had met many of the men who would fill the stage here and he, himself, had become part of this wider scene. My feeling is that he would have been fiercely disappointed. Back in St. Just, to which he must return, would they understand about affairs out here or think him simply a failure?

Only, hey presto! He does not set off home to Cornwall at once.

An Aside.

During my visit to South Africa in 1990 and whilst in Cape Town, I visited the Archives Department in Roebuck Street and there, besides my Grandfather's Will read other papers in his file, trivial but moving (and more of these by and by). One file yielded up the number of a letter sent to the Transvaal authorities in 1879 and

26

when I returned to England I wrote for information. The copy of this letter came to me some months later. This letter from the past confirmed another family tradition that grandfather at some time in his life had 'gone trekking' and this letter was confirmation. And even this year in 1998 has another piece of the same jigsaw come to my notice in the book by the late Richard Dawe. It is called 'Cornish Pioneers in South Africa' and on page 77 is written, "When Francis Oats visited the only gold mine at Pilgrim's Rest in 1874 he found two St. Just men working there" (quoted from The Cornishman, January, 3rd, 1875).

The letter, which I have the copy of, not only revealed that he did go off exploring but also that he did return to South Africa writing this letter in 1879. And the gist of the letter is an offer by him to do a detailed report on the areas he had inspected, but the Transvaal Government turned down his offer.

For myself back in England, my mind kept turning to this trek; his first one must have been undertaken soon after he arrived in Africa. Did he not then go immediately to Kimberley? Did someone ask him to go and perhaps with others? From the second letter, at least, one can follow where he went and also by the letter know that he went on the trip "to inform myself". Did he go alone or perhaps with others who recently lost their jobs? In the vast spaces he could recover from his disappointment and debate the future. This was his third long journey. Now maybe Africa cast her spell on him as on so many, the oxen, the camping, the cries of the 'boys' driving and all the sounds in this still untrammelled land; unhitching in the daytime heat, for the oxen to rest and graze and themselves to sleep. Then to travel on for part of the night.

In his letter he describes briefly the places he went to prospect. The lead mines of Mariso, the cobalt, coal and iron at Middleburg, the gold in the neighbourhood of Eersteling, and to the Blauwberg Range and Marabastad. Some areas he wished to have seen, but he could not as there was a minor war in progress at that time.

On his return to Kimberley, how long did he stay there? Certainly he would have left before the winter set in, the previous one had been very bitter with great snow storms. A strong wind had come one day in July, which blew up clouds of a very "light blue" and by midnight, snow began to fall and stayed many days. It could happen this year too, and delay transport or even stop it from moving. My guess is that he went soon, away to the coast to take a steamer for England.

No. 4, Church Street would be bursting with preparations. Maybe he returned in time for the great festival, St Just Feast, held in November (the closest Sunday to All Saints' Day). At the end of his long travel, the bay and St. Michael's Mount, 'the guarded mount', and the train drawing towards Marazion and terminus at Penzance. Was Elizabeth Ann there on the platform and did they climb together on board the horse-bus? His second journey out of Cornwall was over. Now there were great tales to tell and discussions once more of the future. For the immediate future he settled back at Botallack and in his spare time re-wrote his report for the Colonial Office. I think this must have included possible matters to do with the Transvaal journey.

CHAPTER 4
OPPORTUNITY ONLY KNOCKS ONCE

Mid-Years
 " The Wind is Tugging my sails away
 The Moon is treading my Ship away."

D. H. Lawrence

So 1877 came in with Francis Oats back at Botallack. When did the cable from Kimberley come? Was spring well on? Sufficient that come it did with the offer of a post as mining engineer to the Baring Gould and Atkins Mining Company in the Kimberley Mine. Certain it is that the head of the firm, Francis Baring Gould, and Francis Oats had met in 1875-6. The former was the 4th son of the rector of Lewtrenchard, across from Launceston on the Devon side of the Tamar. He and his brother Edward were early at the diggings and it was their company which was to figure largely in the amalgamation process in later years. Mention of it was made by Anthony Trollope when he visited Kimberley in 1877 towards the end of the year. He noticed it was one of the most prosperous concerns and that the company had been quick to recognise the advantage of co-operative mining. He also noted that they had gone to the expense of sinking a perpendicular shaft with a tunnel below from the shaft to the mine. Was Francis Oats responsible for this work or some of it?

This time on his return, Elizabeth Ann accompanied him; they travelled aboard the steamship *Myanza* and they left the ship at Port Elizabeth. This would mean the journey inland was a shorter one.

There was a sad start to this new life, for on the voyage out, Elizabeth Ann had their first child, still-born. And one wonders much what this bereaved young woman made of the place, which was to be her home for a good many years. One hopes she was made welcome, they were of a certainty Cornish folk, even some from her own parish who would help her settle in. The home was the usual cabin, corrugated iron and with a canvas lining inside and probably only a beaten earth floor, only a few years earlier it would have been a tent. However much Francis had told her, it was all surely very strange. And the township itself with its dust and flies and no piped water. Well, of course in St. Just it had to be hand-pumped, but at least there was no shortage. Sanitation still had to be tackled. Southey had closed the gambling dens and Lanyon more recently had decreased the number of licenses for canteens, the 'drinking halls'. This year too, Kimberley had become a municipality and the newly elected council members quickly had their hands full with problems and more problems.

Even so Kimberley was a lively place to live and became, over the years, a respectable and fine city. Folk had always enjoyed entertainments. The theatre was popular from the start. Under Major Lanyon's instructions the dreary public park had recently been re-laid with fine trees and walks and held tennis courts and a croquet lawn. On Sunday afternoons the band played and the local volunteers paraded from their headquarters near-by. There were two hospitals and horse cabs for hire and later would be buses and trams. Early on, places for worship had been started, first in a tent and later in tin shacks. In 1872, the chapel goers had replaced the tent (blown down during a storm, the canvas actually fell on top of the congregation and they had to crawl out from under!); it was replaced by a wooden and iron building. This was in West End, the district next to the Kimberley mine and where they lived at first. Here, they would have worshipped and went sometimes to promenade in the newly laid out gardens, called then the 'Victoria', with a statue of the Queen presiding. When I came here it had been renamed the 'Queens' Garden' in honour of the visit of Elizabeth II.

A brief report in the Cornish Telegraph of Christmas Eve 1878 notes that Captain Francis Oats, some time agent at Botallack, "has been appointed engineer to the Kimberley Mining Company, South Africa, for £150/month".

Earlier that year comfort must have come stealing into the young couple's hearts as a new life quickened and in 1878 was born another child, named Francis. However this joy was short lived, as he died within the year, probably of enteritis. It was not until 1880 that a baby came who was to thrive and grow. Here too a bit of history takes a hand. The year before from Scotland came a doctor to be partner to Dr. Prince and so it was young Starr Jamieson delivered the son. Jamieson and Francis were to be friends all their lives.

This infant was baptised Francis Freathy, who with his last name conjured up the green valleys of Cornwall with the bright light of Africa. And indeed, Francis Freathy was to know much of Cornwall and of South Africa. At this moment in time he lay in his cradle, his parents peeping down on him. (My own dear father, of course.)

The days and years went by, Francis at the Baring Gould holding in the Kimberley Mine, Elizabeth Ann, a busy mother and housewife. Nothing comes written down from these first years, not even a baby's birth certificate. Not yet did the Kimberley authorities register births. Though once more when I looked through the documents in Cape Town I did unearth a faint sad echo of those days. In 1881 was born another son, Victor. He was to live only into the following year, dying at the Strand Hotel in Somerset West. He was buried in the grave yard of the Dutch Reformed Church. Reading Francis's Will therein are instructions for the grave of this little dead son to be kept tidy and, annually a sum of £3 was sent to this church in payment. No records seem to have been kept, and through the Somerset Authorities, I was informed that the present minister knew nothing.

Anyway what were the Oats doing in this town in 1882? On their way to the coast to take a steamer back to Britain, stopping only for the sad necessity to bury Victor. Back in St. Just, Francis Oats would have stayed maybe a month or so but when he returned to Kimberley he had left his wife and two-year old son for a longer period, perhaps with his mother or with the Olds family. There in the windswept town of her birth, Elizabeth Ann had another son whom she had christened Wilfred, in spite of a cable from her husband with a long list of other names. Perhaps it was a fashionable

29

name just then!

In 1884, the family was reunited and that same year moved house to live in the popular area called Belgravia. It remains a pleasant suburb of Kimberley and not so close to the mines and the market as the earlier home. Here successful men built fine colonial-style houses, with a wealth of handsome wrought iron gates and fences and verandas surrounded by well-laid out gardens. Where the Oats had their home is not recorded, nor whether he had it built or bought a place from someone moving.

Francis in 1883 had left the Baring Gould company and was now the mining engineer for the Victoria Company. He became, as time went on, the chief shareholder in this company and as such had a full say in their policy making. The manager of the mine was Rudolf Hinrichsen.

In the Belgravia home was born yet another boy, this time called Giles, a good family one this time, and in 1886 came the daughter, Elise, to complete the family in fine style. In this year too, specimens of gold-bearing rock were brought down from the Witswatersrand in the Northern Transvaal. Soon there would be an exodus from Kimberley and fortunes made in diamonds taken north to be used to found even greater ones in the new gold mines. Francis did not re-establish himself. He was not so interested in gold, it seems, nor did he invest much in those mines. Later he used often to go to the Rand and Johannesburg quite frequently on business for the De Beers Company. If Cornish miners there knew he was travelling up they would often meet his train in order to speak with him or ask his advice about some mining matter. Francis Oats remained ever a Cornishman and as for Elizabeth Ann, I feel she never liked Kimberley and couldn't wait to go back to Cornwall!

Something of Victoria

The Victoria Company was eventually taken over by the De Beers Mining Company, run by Rhodes and Rudd, in 1887-8 by the policy of secretly buying up shares and becoming the majority holders. Rhodes' policy was to destroy all records of mines he bought out but there are details remaining which throw a light on the Victoria. One has to do with a strike. In 1882 the Diamond Trade Act was passed. Under this law, white workers, as well as black, were to undergo searching (for possible theft of diamonds). It was the cause of almost immediate unrest and suspicion by the white overseers, mechanics and engine drivers. They went on strike in 1883 and did not return to work until the mine managers agreed to no stripping for white workers.

Soon afterward, the French Company and then the Central sacked some of their engine drivers and mechanics. In 1884, the Bulfontien Mining Company stripped white workers. Next day a mass meeting was held. It was decided to send a telegram to the Governor of the Cape, followed by a petition signed by 2,000 men asking for a suspension of the stripping clause. Next in this troubled time the mine owners of De Beers and the French Company announced they would lock out workers who did not wear regulation clothing and search officers were to search every fifth man. No one would submit and at the end of the shift they were sacked. There was an immediate reaction. Mine whistles blew, the sign of an immediate strike. A huge meeting was held on the racecourse. The strike committee warned men not to approach the mining companies which were still at work but on the following day there was a big crowd assembled on the waste tips near the Victoria Mine. The newspaper said the manager came out to talk to them and his name was Francis Oats. However then he was still just the mining engineer. He had a long discussion with them and it was agreed to suspend all operations until noon the following day.

Meanwhile the French Company was responsible for keeping the pumps going for the whole of the Kimberley Mine. If the mine was flooded the men would at once be thrown out of work. Eventually the strikers arrived to stop the pumps and force was resorted to by them. The guards retaliated by firing, killing four miners and wounding others. People were shocked and great numbers turned out for the funerals. And by and by the strikers drifted back to work.

After this the mine owners pressed for compounds to be set up. But this, like matters to do with the illicit diamond trade, was another much debated subject and it comes up again and again and not until all the mining companies were under one head was it finally decided. I have put this about the strikes to show how complex diamond mining had become and how involved Francis Oats must have been.

Returning to actual mining to extract the diamonds, in 1885 Francis sank a shaft in the Victoria Mine and in 1964 it was decided to de-water the shaft (which had been long unused) and re-open it. It was used for a time and then gradually fell out of use again. I was taken to see Rhodes' old original office by the mining engineer, and he quite casually suggested I looked at the old Victoria Shaft which was near at hand. It moved me very much looking on this long ago creation of my grandfather.

Back to the 1880s Rhodes was at pains to buy up as many claims as he could and in the Kimberley mines the same ideas were to prevail. From the early days of his arrival here as the Mining Inspector for the colonial government, Francis Oats had understood clearly that eventually, for ease of production, the many small holdings would need to be bought out and that amalgamation was the only answer.

But when it became the turn of Victoria to be targeted he did not make it easy to take! He had to do his best for the shareholders and he and Hinrichsen put up a good fight. The company was well-run and production fair. It was only then that Rhodes had to resort to his usual under-hand ways and arranged with Beit's connivance to buy shares secretly on the London market and so not arouse suspicion in Kimberley. It was because the majority of shares were held between these two men that Rhodes could openly approach Victoria and in 1887-8, the company was liquidated. Letters are still extant in which Rhodes writes of the need for secrecy, "we don't want to upset Oats yet" and "we are not ready to tackle Oats yet".

One odd matter is also recorded. As early as 1884, Stow (Rhodes' 'undercover' man in London) almost succeeded in landing the important Victoria Mining Company into the De Beers net. However his powers of negotiation were suddenly cancelled by cable. The failure to secure the company then cost the De Beers concern a great deal more money at the later date. To me it remains a mystery. Was it the first hiccup in the rift which later separated these two players for high stakes?

However with the Victoria bought out and only two small concerns to be liquidated, the De Beers company owned the whole of the mine and got ready to battle for supremacy with the Kimberley mining companies. Francis Oats was given a seat on the board and from his erstwhile shareholders a bonus of £6,500 and as a further mark of their appreciation they presented him with an 18-carat gold lever watch and his wife Elizabeth-Ann with a gold watch and chain. Soon after these events Francis and his family left for Europe. Again dates are unsure of when they started their journey. Francis had a place on the old De Beers Mining Company, but it was soon to change its name and its status. He was in St. Just when the huge fire broke out in the De Beers mine and a cable was sent to tell him. Two St. Just men had died and he must have known them. Another record of his presence in West Penwith comes in the news he was buying more shares in Levant Mine in 1887 and of matters at the shareholders meeting when he was present and into the next years.

The huge excavation of Kimberley Diamond Mine.

It was on March 12th 1888 that the new company in Kimberley was formed and henceforward called the De Beers Consolidated Mines Ltd. Its immediate and chief object was to further the interests in the sale of diamonds, but this company with Rhodes at its head could not be any ordinary one. When the mine was taken over Francis was retired as manager of the Victoria Company.

By its trust deeds it had immense and diverse powers and became a most useful weapon in Rhodes' climb to power. As he often said "One cannot carry out great schemes if there is no money to finance them", and his eyes were turned more and more to the north. Enclosed here by Dr. Buys, the archivist of De Beers, are the details of the powers that could be wielded by the company and it was soon to be seen how these were used for Rhodes' schemes for expansion into the north, to vast lands over which to wave a Union Jack. The settlement on the areas to the north, ruled by the Matebele and the Mashonas and soon to be named Rhodesia, was largely achieved through the support of the company. All the money borrowed was repaid in a very short time as Rhodes was always delighted to tell the shareholders.

At the second annual general meeting of De Beers, Henry Robinson was in the chair and at the re-election of the directors, two new ones were elected, Francis Oats and Julius Wernher. And soon after this date the Oats family must have taken up residence in Belgravia again and of course, from now onward, Francis was to faithfully serve this company to the end of his life. Kimberley too, became an even more unique place sending money and expertise up to the goldfields and the foundation of Johannesburg. Volunteers trained here and then went north to defend the new acquisitions. When two Kimberley mines, Dutoitspan and Bulfontein, closed down, workers there were offered land up there to settle on. Those who did not go took to debris washing, or lived on their savings or left Kimberley. No longer was there a place for the individual, only within the De Beers Consolidated Mining Company Limited was there stability. The old competitive days were gone. Kimberley became staider and perhaps a steadier place. Better roads and buildings attested to the assured security and the growing wealth of the company. Rhodes put into operation his fine plans to build workers better homes and Kenilworth village was laid out – a kind of early garden suburb.

Another matter of great urgency for the company came up when diamonds were found on Wesselton Farm, near the town. People hoped it would be declared a public digging but after protracted negotiations it was bought by De Beers. Diggers and their supporters held a mass meeting against the take-over. But the overriding policy, across the years, was to remain the same, and that was that diamonds for the market must be strictly controlled. Prices could not be maintained if sales were not limited, hence the buying up of this farm to control production.

In 1890 came the Governor of the Cape, Sir Henry Lock and his wife and, of course, they were given a true Kimberley welcome in spite of the financial difficulties of some. Receptions and parties followed each other, culminating with a great ball in the Kimberley Club.

In 1891, Barney Barnato was in the Chair at the De Beers annual meeting, and talk of diamonds was mixed with plans for the South African International Exhibition to be held in Kimberley in 1892. Barnato said "It would be in their interests to show the world their diamonds, their methods of working....in fact the whole economy and method of an industrial and financial corporation which had not its equal in the whole world."

In 1892, Francis Oats took the chair for the first time for his new company. The working of De Beers, the growth of Kimberley and the Cape and its policies, all are part and parcel of Francis Oats' life and important to him and he was to rub shoulders with many a person much mentioned in history. The years up to the outbreak of the Anglo-Boer War were increasingly busy for him and in all his life onward, so much better recorded than his early life, he seems never to have been still!

In harness for De Beers he seemed happy and enthusiastic seeing to the interests of the Company. There were the general meetings and the important annual one and consultations always with the office in London. He journeyed far to prospect for them, or inspect a new place or property. When the International Exhibition was in the city did he, I wonder, cast his mind back to the Paris of twenty five years ago, when as a lad he had set off with £10 in his pocket and had seen Kimberley diamonds for the first time and the replica of the first great South African diamond, the Eureka!

Rhodes, as often as he could escape the cares of Prime Minister, came up through Kimberley on his way north. On one of these visits, the directors living in Kimberley held a meeting with him in his carriage. Again, the opulent touch, on the White Train specially built carriages from America were drawn, used for De Beers directors and for visitors to their company, every up-to-date equipment was installed, and can be viewed in the museum on Kimberley old mine today, from a table laid fully with linen and silver to the whiskey in the cut glass decanters! (I have an evocative old photograph of my mother (see page 78), her hair in a high coif and wearing an elegant long skirt in 1912, standing outside this carriage, in which she had travelled up from Cape Town, to visit her father-in-law and show him his first grandson, still an infant.)

But in 1895 all the stability was disrupted, it is the time for the infamous Jamieson raid and in 1896 came the capture of him and his men and of the 'Reformers' in Johannesburg. This was an attempt by the force of another country to persuade Paul Kruger (President of the Boer Republic) to give the Uitlanders (outsiders or foreigners) a vote and more liberal government. This sorry episode had far reaching consequences, fuelling antagonism between Boer and Briton. All too soon a full scale war was to put paid to any attempts at reconciliation, or to alter the Transvaal franchise by peaceful means.

Rhodes never was to recover from this disgrace, he being implicitly involved in this unlawful attempt to interfere with another government. He resigned and henceforward was in opposition, calling his party the Progressives. As he no longer had the confidence of the Afrikaaner or Bond party he had to find others to vote for him and he resorted to almost any means, even to bribing black men to vote for him (there were, I understand a percentage of votes allowed to these people and certainly the Cape Coloureds - mixed race - were allowed votes then).

The way Rhodes got many people into parliament was dirty and this is a part of Francis Oats' career, I do not like. He, himself, I am sure did not stoop to such methods but the fact remains into the House of Assembly he arrived in 1898. John Xavier Merriman, an Englishman from Somerset, who had come as a boy to the Colony with his parents was for very many years an Independent member of Parliament for Namaqualand West. Rhodes lavished money and paid an agent from Britain to run his campaign. The agent's method of bribery or intimidation won over voters and Merriman's seat was no longer a safe one for him and he finally went elsewhere. This area was very arid, with scattered farms and mining communities busy with the extraction of copper. Whilst in Kimberley I asked the Head Librarian, Mrs. Leslie Brits, if there were any details about this election, but nothing very spectacular came forth in the local press, and the Cape Times simply stated that Mr. Oats, the Progressive Party's candidate, the Junior Member for Namaqualand, polled almost double the number of votes cast for the unsuccessful Bond candidate.

It certainly makes the thinly veiled animosity between Merriman and Francis Oats understandable when they were contending across the floor of the House of Assembly. It is only too clear Merriman saw Oats as a Rhodes supporter and a trampler down of principles, a worshipper of power and money. Francis Oats looked on Merriman as a traitor to Britain, as a renegade. He was to taunt across the floor towards the government benches, "I am a Britisher!"

I myself, have a great admiration for John Merriman, who stood in the central stream of politics, wanting the best way forward for both Dutch and British under the Union Jack. During his life he was much maligned.

My cousin, Mrs. Ann Gilchrist, granddaughter too of Francis through his daughter Elise, told me she had never found much in Hansard in the way of speeches by him, mostly ' Oh, oh's' or 'Rubbish' during debates. I was luckier during my short time in the Library of the Parliament in Cape Town, maybe because before leaving England, I had written to the Head Librarian and on arrival was quickly presented with the necessary volumes to inspect. Even so, I could only dig out a limited amount of debates and certainly did not cover the eight years he was a member of the House of Assembly.

Although the first report I did trace had only one sentence by Francis, it was on a matter to do with a coal merchant's petition. The rest of the members gave lengthy discussions, he simply said "The Petition should be dismissed!" and in the end it was thrown out! The other matters on which he spoke at some length, both on the floor and in committee, were about the building of railways, bridges, dams for irrigation and such like - projects to forward the opening up of this vast land with easier and cheaper transport and to have more storage of water for crops in times of scarce rainfall.

In the backbiting debates to do with the Vryburg voters, he does his best to defend Rhodes, who was accused of 'whiskey swilling!' Francis stood up and spoke of Rhodes as a "most abstemious gentleman". Presumably he must have had his tongue in his cheek knowing that Rhodes was a heavy drinker!

Then there were the equally unpleasant debates. Merriman was the Treasurer for the Government. When Oats brought up the plight of the poor farmers in Namaqualand he, Merriman, had some cutting remarks to say to him about his concern. He dubs Francis "Mr. Oats, the omnipotent member for Namaqualand", adding the fact that the farmers had not voted for him!

I have read the lives of Rhodes, Merriman and Scheiner, who was Prime Minister at this troubled time. One is cast into a welter of politics, political parties, personalities, loyalties and one can only dimly struggle to visualise the stage upon which these men walked and for a while Francis Oats too.

So many books have been written about Cecil Rhodes and if one does not believe such travesties as the recent film of him, so much the better. He was a strange dynamic man with dreams of world power for Britain believing fervently this country had the most to offer. Francis Oats met him on the first visit to Kimberley and certainly they met and worked together. Family tradition says that Francis never feared Rhodes and always spoke his mind.

However from the minutes of the De Beers meetings it comes across that, at least in the policies to do with diamonds and their sale and the restriction on their sale when necessary to keep up prices, Francis carried out the ideas of his chairman and continued to do so when he became chairman in 1908.

But were they ever close except as business men? Socially they mixed but Francis is never mentioned in the crowd about Rhodes. I think their backgrounds were too different, Rhodes coming from a comfortably settled middle-class family, sending their sons to University or into professions, but Francis was self-made, from working class people. Rhodes' family was Anglicans and a Wesleyan background ruled in the main through the Olds connection in Francis Oats' family. Probably just another of my hunches, but 1 feel the two worked in harness together but did not 'play' together.

CHAPTER 5
A CORNISH ASIDE

Cornish mining

The 1890s was a dark time for Cornish mining. Cornish mines could not deal with the glut of cheap, foreign, tin on the market and many closed although many struggled on. Botallack Mine had been failing for many years prior to its closure. At a shareholder's meeting at the end of 1894 Francis said that he had "invested more out of regard to the locality than anything else". Early the following year the mine was laying men off preparatory to closing. Francis offered (he was back in South Africa at the time) to take up 5,000 shares if the mine were to be restarted in 50,000 or 100,000 shares. Unfortunately there was little or no support from the other major shareholders on such a dubious proposal.

But with Levant it was very different, I feel he had a love/hate relationship here, not with the old mine but with the old-fashioned approach by other adventurers or shareholders. Over the years he spent much time and energy trying to get the mine run by more modern methods and at the end he lost heart. In 1915 both he and his son suggested the closure of the mine (and maybe its tragic latter history would have been thus avoided). If one has time to read the mine reports and for an excellent overall picture to read the story of the mine by Cyril Noall one cannot be unaware that Francis Oats wanted changes. He did prevail sometimes, such as the building of a dry for the men and the tunnel from the Man Engine Shaft, so that they changed into warm clothes etc.. without going into the cold air at surface. The adventurers meetings were attended by the press so most matters came to public view, unless as happens the press add their editor's bias!

One of the matters very much the wish of Francis to alter was the old out-dated cost book system to one of limited liability, or at least to have money set aside in times of success for a 'rainy day'. But to no avail. As long as members could jog along, enjoy the 'count' dinners and a glass or two of grog, the future was not much bothered about. A saying by one of the older members, when the failing resources of the mine were under discussion, was "Oh, there's enough in the old place yet to see us out," advocating the taking out the best stuff and blow those who come later. Such men must have been anathema to Francis. Doubtless he must have rubbed many the wrong way! He pulled no punches! When he tried to force through some of his ideas one shareholder complained that 'the large shareholders were having the whole voice in the business matters'. Captain Oats replied with some slighting remarks about small shareholders who were only in and out of a mine!

Later in this meeting he said he thought the mine captains were not paid enough and considering the responsibility, they had received less than any other mine he knew of. He considered the way the tin was sold from Levant as unfair and tried to get it altered, why was not the tin ore sold by ticket as at other mines going to the highest bidder and so enriching the mine from where it came? He was well aware that some of the bigger shareholders were merchants and bankers who paid a fixed sum for all the ore produced.

He also had the temerity to suggest that the committee was unnecessary and that an efficient mine-manager could run Levant on his own! Needless to say the members did not like this suggestion and voted each other on again for a further sixteen weeks! Francis said he was not against any one individual but he said he did not think it right for the members to sign each others cheques and pass each others bill, nor should there be so many merchants on the committee!

To leave Levant on a less abrasive note, let us mention Mr. H. Tippett. He was known as Herbert and was a skilled engine-driver and for many years drove the traction engine at Levant. The family lived in Cot Valley and I knew his daughters, Gertrude and Mercia, when first one and then the other lived at the old farm, Carrallack. Mr. Gerrish was famed for his wonderful pedigree Guernseys, taking prizes out of Cornwall and selling his dairy cattle not only at the big Reading auctions but to customers abroad, and if he was noted for these fine animals, Mrs. Gerrish was equally famed for her open house. To think on her table takes me back to far off young days, groaning under its weight of Cornish dishes and, of course, huge wide bowls of crusty yellow cream, (it used then to be called scald cream) Mercia came to join her sister and now her two daughters are coming back to live in the old farmhouse.

Several years ago John Corin kindly escorted me to Levant to see for the first time the old beam whim restored to pristine condition and smoothly working. Here I met a small man who told me that my grandfather, on one of his trips back from Kimberley, said to his grandfather, "I have a place for you out in Africa". Francis Oats knew a good miner and would be glad to offer a job to suit him if one was available.

Francis Oats was also a major shareholder in Wheal Basset which was also in financial problems, along with the adjacent mines, in the 1890s. In 1896 it was decided to amalgamate Wheal Basset with South Wheal Francis and work both as Basset Mines Ltd. (in 1910 Francis Freathy was also listed as a director). There is plenty of evidence in local papers and letters to some papers about his chairmanship and again it is found that he chaffed against the non-instalment of modern machinery, the main purpose of which was to lessen the costs of running a mine. A part of a letter about his speech to shareholders brings out this point, quoted, 'Francis never felt happy if the best use was not forthcoming for continued working improvements and he felt that men were inclined to rest on their laurels'. After all, he knew only too well how much a good miner could achieve in a working day.

Letter from a reader.

"The letter from Captain Oats in yesterday's West Briton, deserves more than a passing notice and I was greatly disappointed in not seeing his speech at Wheal Basset on the need of improved machinery and intelligent engineering in the work of our mines more fully reported. Captain Oats spoke for about 40 minutes on the subject in the most intelligent and convincing manner, his remarks being most opportune. I find that he does not deny but that there have been great additions to our mining machinery, and more especially at Carn Brea, to the tune of £40,000 in 7 years but from the tone of his letter, he evidently doubts the improvements. If this is his meaning I entirely agree with him, for a more deplorable state of things than mining engineering in comparison with that applied to shipping and other commercial undertakings can scarcely be imagined. The whole system is rotten to the core; the object seems to be instead of economy in the use of fuel, to use as much as possible."

Other interests were in the Bissoe Valley where ochre was found and in the Bickford-Smith fuse and explosive factories. On one of these visits Francis presented the Lafrowda Institute, St Just, where once he had attended lectures and had been Curator, with a portrait of Sir Clement Le Neve Foster, the mining engineer and former Inspector of Mines, who as a young man, had instructed him so well and encouraged him in his studies. Francis Oats always acknowledged any success he may have achieved in later life was due to this man, who, eminent in his profession, was to become Professor Foster.

The minutes recorded a letter of thanks to him but this portrait has long since disappeared, no one knows where. So in Cornwall the mines held him, and on the domestic front also. Once the children reached schooling age Francis and Elizabeth Ann must have decided they were to be educated in Britain. Their eldest son, Freathy, had been at school in this country for a long time, first in Fowey where probably he could lodge with relatives and in 1895 by the date in a Book Prize, he was at

Levant Mine on the St Just cliffs.

39

school in Jersey. (A lady from this island who became a friend of ours years later has told me she remembers the school, although when she was a girl there it had become a private house.) Whilst the Oats children were younger they were taught in Kimberley by a resident governess. One whose name 1 have heard was a French lady, Madam Birst.

There is a family hand-down that Francis paid her, or perhaps another, too much attention and Elizabeth Ann took off in dudgeon for Australia to stay with her brothers and was gone for six months! Be that as it may, the children grew and needed schools. So it was that in 1892, when Rhodes was buying his great house under the Mountain in Cape Town, in a small way Francis was up-grading his family living by buying 4, Market Street, later known as Carne House, to be a permanent St. Just home for them all. Before, one can only guess they stayed with his mother or mother-in-law or with relatives. Now they could come and go, with Carne House a warm comfortable place, as I have been told, and home for many years.

CHAPTER 6
SOUTH AFRICAN PROBLEMS

Kimberley and De Beers Concerns Prior to the Outbreak of War 1899

The decade ended in war, a grievous and quite unwarranted war with Milner, the chief architect. "It will only be a little war", he cabled to Joseph Chamberlain, the Colonial Secretary. What a future of bitterness he unleashed and how incorrect he was about the length. But much happened in Kimberley before October 1899 saw them besieged.

In 1897, two shocking happenings. News came of the drowning of Barney Barnato, Life Governor of De Beers, who was on board a ship returning to England. It was understood he committed suicide but at the inquiry even more mystery seemed to surround his death. He was, of course, an influential figure in Johannesburg and involved in many gold mining companies.

Nearer home a terrible scourge arrived. Rhodes had had cattle sent up from Cape farms to his newly acquired territories in the North and they were infected with the disease called rinderpest. It was a disease endemic in the land but this decade the outbreaks were many and serious. To stem the disease the Cape Parliament decreed not only should the infected animals be destroyed but the rest of the herds involved.

The black man's wealth had always been in cattle. Unrest was immediate and the Matebele rose in rebellion and very grave it was with isolated white farming families being killed. When the Matebele were partially defeated they retired to their mountain fastnesses. Now Rhodes was to have his finest hour. Courage he did not lack. He went to meet the tribal chiefs unarmed and agreement was reached. He forbade retribution.

Unfortunately, near Kimberley the tribe ruled by Galishiwe revolted against the order to slaughter their cattle. This rebellion was subdued by Colonel David Harris, who was in charge of the Kimberley Volunteers.

The rinderpest decimated the herds, including those raised on the De Beers farms. As a company it was agreed that they should invite the eminent German scientist, Dr. Koch to come out to try to find a cure. He was given every facility by the company and the use of the old Victoria Mine's washing floors to carry out his experiments. Eventually he found an antidote and this brilliant man was awarded the Nobel Prize in 1905.

Another outcome of the decimation of the herds was naturally a great shortage of meat. De Beers had hundreds of workers to feed. They decided to set up refrigerating plants, one in Cape Town and the second in Kimberley. Special trains pulled cold storage trucks and the import of meat from Australia and New Zealand was set in hand.

In Kimberley itself a fire destroyed the old Town Hall and so in 1898 the foundation stone was laid for an imposing new building. It was opened in September, 1899, so was just in time for the last fete before hostilities broke out and during the siege

Francis Oats Francis in the uniform of the Kimberley Defence Force
during the Boer War. Taken at Kimberley in 1899

Young Francis Freathy in the uniform of the South African
Light Horse during the first Boer War

the grand building housed refugees from the surrounding farms and settlements. However, it remains in the centre of Kimberley today and looks very well. More matters in which De Beers had interests and invested money and so in which Francis Oats also was involved over the years.

Dynamite was necessary in great quantities for both the diamond and the gold mines. There was a factory in the Transvaal but the "unduly high prices charged them was a very great burden," said Rhodes. De Beers also imported dynamite from Europe (from Nobel), also at very high prices. So plans were set in motion to build a plant for themselves. Gardner Williams, (now retired mine manager of the De Beers Mines) himself an American, persuaded a fellow countryman to come and work for the company. R. W. Quinan was an expert in this field and he came over to choose a site and it was to be in Somerset West. Francis Oats had been a director of a new explosives company in Cornwall, the British and Colonial Explosives Company, based at Perranporth. This had been set up in 1889, intending to supply explosives to De Beers. Unfortunately it was never successful and was taken over by Nobel's in 1893, having never sold any explosives to Africa.

The Anglo-Boer war delayed the factory's completion, but by 1903 it was in production and from then on all De Beers explosives were supplied from here with a great saving of costs. Later on in 1910, when Quinan's son had taken over the management he suggested that the company invest in a glycerine factory so as to make them independent of imported refined glycerine. It was built by 1914, "Just in time, otherwise we should have to continue to buy from Holland and we might have been in great difficulties," said Francis Oats.

Coal was also of major importance to the mines and needed in great amounts to drive the steam engines and it was also linked inextricably with the building of railways. At his first time in Kimberley, Francis had noted the coal used was of poor quality and also hard to transport. As the mines deepened the need to fuel the machines became greater, hence he was always so insistent on more and more railways to be laid. And De Beers loaned the Government money to help in such projects. The inferior coal used to come from Indewe across the border in the Transvaal but later he helped pioneer the finding and opening of fields in Natal, which once exploited proved sufficient to rely on.

Francis had little connection with gold other than through the company with the Rand gold fields, though in his will he had some shares in a mine there, but he went up to look at gold prospects at Rhodes' request in the new territories, land there had been given to the company in exchange for money loans. In June 1899, Francis was in Mashonaland returning in time to Kimberley to be shut up there in October.

The first manager of the second company was John Blades Currey. It was he who was in charge of the South African replica diamond, the Eureka, in Paris in 1867. Francis was to meet him in 1874-5 because he was the Colonial Secretary to Southey in Kimberley. Later Currey built a house in Belgravia called 'The Lodge', now a museum, and so he and Francis ended up near neighbours. De Beers had interests in this company and as we have seen these miners tipped the scales in favour of the Junior Member, Francis Oats!

In August, 1884 a small naval detachment raised the German flag over South West Africa and in November a British military expedition annexed Bechuanaland to the Crown. Earlier in a Kimberley newspaper attention was drawn to a new mineral prospectors had found, crocidolite or woolly stone, all through the Kuruman Hills (also known as the Asbestos Mountains). The article commented "it is to be hoped that too much of this valuable article will not be discovered and glut the market!" Three years later a Kimberley speculator, Cohen, inspected the asbestos samples from the Prieska area brought to the diamond fields by labourers. He showed these samples "to the most knowledgeable mining man in Kimberley", Francis Oats. He was interested and visited Prieska. In 1891 he created the Cape Mineral Syndicate and prepared to buy or lease farms near Koegas and begin exporting to Europe. There were many difficulties before production and export got underway and too long to put in all details. Of course, the mining stopped during the Anglo-Boer War.

There were grave droughts, lack of oxen for transport owing to the rinderpest and the long distances to be travelled to the ports. Also there were manufacturing problems. This blue asbestos was a harder substance than the white fluffy stuff used up to this time in Europe. The descriptions and quotes above come from an excellent book by Anthony Hocking (a Cornishman surely?) called "Kaias and Cocopans, A History of Mining in South Africa's Northern Cape". Another interesting family fact came through a glimpse at this book, Rundle Olds was manager of the mine, and he was nephew to Francis. Rundle was Maria's son and his family were later to settle in Rhodesia.

Regarding tin, all I know at this date is that Francis Oats prospected for tin in Swaziland but it was the McCreedy Tin Mines which exploited the deposits. I am possessed of an oil painting which shows my grandfather with panning shovel and busy above a river in a mountainous looking terrain in the country of Swaziland. An alert black boy is squatting near, further towards the water is Francis Freathy bending over and searching too, and a disconsolate son (Giles) loafing on the further side of his father.

Kimberley During the Siege, 1899-1900

" There are no stars tonight
But those of memory. Yet how much room for memory there is
In the loose girdle of soft rain....."
Hart Crane from 'My Grandmother's Love Letters'

As to the siege of the town in which Francis was with two other directors, and Rhodes too, I have left it to be told more or less from the diary of Miles Henderson, son of the mayor at the commencement of the hostilities and the siege came very swiftly after the Transvaal declared war. Of Rhodes I will dwell on as little as possible, he having boarded the last train up from Cape Town. He had no need to come and, of course, was himself, trying to order all things if he could, doing good actions, and bad ones and making himself thoroughly obnoxious to the commander in charge Colonel Robert Kekewich (of the Loyal North Lancashire Regiment). But there are plenty of history books which cover this subject in detail.

Early on Francis Oats sent a cable to Clifton College in Bristol asking the headmaster to "send my sons out to fight." The reply was to allow the eldest son to join up, but mentioning that the other two were too young! Francis Freathy, then 19 years old, arrived in Cape Town and was drafted into the South African Light Horse (also known as the "Reformer's Regiment", Winston Churchill also served with this unit). He and his father must have been in touch once the Kimberley siege was lifted but no letters exist from this time. Francis Freathy was with the relieving troops sent to Ladysmith.

In Kimberley, Francis Oats, like most able-bodied men, enlisted in the Town

Guard and they were trained under Colonel Kekewich's orders. One ridiculous, but true, piece of family story comes to light. Also in the defending forces was Rundle Olds, Francis' nephew. When he was on guard duty he had occasion to challenge Francis and asked for the password. But he had forgotten it. In the end an exasperated Francis burst out with "I'm your Uncle Frank! Don't be such a fool!"

Once the siege was raised people were hard at work repairing damage but the mines did not return to full production for some time. The railway had been blown up and the war was still in progress so that coal could not be got straight away, nor a full contingent of black labourers and many of the white younger workers were in the forces.

But in a limited way, Kimberley returned to normal. Food was brought in. The mayor was busy arranging celebrations and fêting for the soldiery. General French was thanked and given a sword! And the displaced Colonel Kekewich (sacked by General French on Rhodes' prompting) was remembered in July, with thanks and a sword and even a cigarette case patterned with diamonds from the Kimberley ladies! And, of course, Rhodes had his portrait painted and it was presented to the Beaconsfield Council. And Jamieson putting the raid disgrace behind him and his charms to the fore, was returned triumphantly for the City Parliament. After the De Beers annual general meeting, Francis Oats went down to Cape Town and early in 1901 he sailed for Europe.

CHAPTER 7
TRAVELS ACROSS THE ATLANTIC

Venture To South America In The Year 1901

At the end of the siege of Kimberley in 1900 Francis Oats would have, with his fellow directors, set about getting the mine back into production as far as possible. The war continued in the north. Coal used to be sent down from Natal by rail, so the task was not easy.

Later in the year he would have gone down to Cape Town to attend the Parliamentary session and perhaps the newly elected Dr. Jamieson joined him in the travelling down. It was a distraught session with difficult decisions to be made for a country coming to the end of a terrible conflict, made more so in that for some, it had been more like a civil war. Towards the close of the year Francis took the chair at the Annual General Meeting of the company back in Kimberley, and all such speeches are all in the archives of De Beers in that town. Soon afterwards he was packing his bags and left for Europe on the SS *Briton* in January 1901.

After over two years and more and much a time of stress he must have been much looking forward to the company of his family, and if not relaxing much, because his life-style seemed never that way inclined, he could change diamond mining problems for those of tin and copper. His elder son, Francis Freathy, was soon to be discharged from the South African forces and to return to Britain, after which he was expected to take up his studies at the Freiberg School of Mines.

However, as it turned, out Francis was to have no prolonged spell in Cornwall nor was his son to get to Germany this year. Soon after his arrival in England, Francis saw an article in the magazine, the Mining Journal, referring to the finding of diamonds in British Guiana. The policy of De Beers had always been to try to keep the diamond market stable. If it became flooded by these gems, the prices would fall and all producers suffer. The upshot was he wrote to the board of directors in London and they in turn alerted the Kimberley board. From the latter came a request from Rhodes, would he consent to go out to British Guiana for them to investigate?

So it fell that when matters were arranged Francis left for South America, taking his son Francis with him as a companion. Almost at the last moment he was asked to include Brazil to report on diamond production there too. May found them on the high seas and on the 10th the ship arrived in Barbados and on the 12th they landed at Georgetown. It was the start of a gruelling six months for the travellers, especially for Francis Oats.

He sent back official reports to the board and more personal details to the Secretary in Kimberley. All these I was able to read whilst in Kimberley in 1989, but long before this time I had known about this journey. When my aunt Ethel Olds died I was given a little booklet of hers, only it turned out not into a book but a container

47

The route taken by Francis and Freathy across South America

of postcards. Freathy, my father, was Ethel's cousin and he sent her these cards from every place, almost, that he and his father visited during their journeys. Back in June, 1901 Francis writes "It is a sleepy place. We went to call on the Governor and the Inspector of Mines today". It was arranged they would go by boat up the River Barima from Bartika (Bartico) to a Mr. Condrad's concession. "Nothing was ready and no one in a hurry!! We are in the middle of a rainy season, raining more or less everyday. One says if the river is up that it is better for the boats but worse for us as at times we have to wade in the water, one cannot walk along the banks, these forests are not like the South African Veldt. I thought Cape Colony up to 20 years ago was the most slow of any, but here nothing in the way of roads, or even paths, let alone railways have been made by the Government to open up the country, and the rivers

48

above the tidal part are almost impassable owing to falls and rapids."

In the end they did get away and travelled for many days and did not return to Georgetown for 38 days. His report was very detailed, but there was no threat to De Beers or the world markets, there were few diamonds and the journeys to export them so tremendous also.

As there was no steamer to Trinidad until August 8th he wrote, "I am using this time to proceed up the Esquibo (Essequibo) River to the Potare tributary, one then travels on the Demara River. A launch goes up the river to diggings on the Onrai and Pantine creeks where gold and diamonds are found. I was told of a claim not on this landing and we took pains to visit it. It was called Green Heart and was worked by two negroes called Magin and Budia. But again only in the gold debris were a few diamonds found. Whilst I was in the Potare district I saw an occurrence of gold in rock, not alluvial, where about 40 black men are engaged in mining and grinding the stone. This is done by hand between two stones, just like the ancients did in Rhodesia."

His reports can all be seen in the De Beers archives, so I will conclude this part of his journey in his own words. "So ended my investigations of the diamond mines of British Guiana. Had I not come up to these almost inaccessible places, or some one from the company, I think it is probable that speculators around must have made a great newspaper cry about the diamond finds here."

Malaria, Tin and Mountain Sickness

On August 8th Francis and his son duly embarked for Trinidad and on arrival had time to visit the famed pitch lakes before they took a steamer for Colon, to cross the Isthmus to Panama. Unfortunately the health of Francis had deteriorated in the torrid forests of British Guiana – he had contracted malaria. Between the diamonds of that place and those of Brazil he had much to endure and his health was never as robust again. In his own words he tells his fellow directors, "On arrival in Panama I was completely prostrate and but for my son's valuable aid I am afraid I should never have got away from there. As it was he got me aboard a Pacific steamer for Mellando and on board was a doctor.....after 10 days the fever left me".

In September, they arrived in Arequipa (in Peru) which is about 150 miles inland and 9,000 feet above sea level. They had a five day wait before catching the train and then the weekly steamer across Lake Titicaca. But before they left Arequipa it was the turn of his son to fall very ill with mountain sickness. After this bout he was never to be so troubled by heights again.

Crossing the great lake to La Paz (Bolivia) here it was Francis's turn to suffer with mountain sickness and he was to continue to suffer very badly from the high altitudes throughout the long journeys in the mountains. The reason for all this overland travel was to look at the tin mining areas, of course of great interest to both with their own involvement in Cornwall's mines. The idea too was to lay a sort of smoke screen so that the public through the newspaper would be less aware of the presence of a De Beers director "snooping about in diamond diggings!"

Because of Francis's sickness being so bad, it was decided to abandon a tremendously long trek to see the famous Potosi tin mine. It would have meant three days on mule back, rising to 16,000 feet with no accommodation and in bitter cold. Instead they took the coach to Santa Cruz but on the way Francis was so ill that he begged to the coachman to leave him behind at one halt. This he fortunately refused to do and on arrival at Oruro a doctor was found to attend to his passenger. Here he writes, "I managed with much resting to visit 4 or 5 of the chief tin producing centres, going as high as 16,000 feet in some places."

Show this card to Percy & tell him that nearly all travelling done here is either in a coach like this one or

Salida de la Diligencia de La Paz al lago Titi-Caca

on a mule's back F. F. O.

Post card sent by Francis Freathy Oats to his cousin Ethel Olds at St Just
with the message "show this card to Percy & tell him that nearly all
travelling done here is either in a coach like this or on a mule's back. F. F. O."

Poor grandfather, on the next stage of their journey, 620 miles by train to Antofagasta, he suffered with neuralgia and was unable to eat. Fortunately the town is at sea level and he recovered. It is only recently that people suffering from mountain sickness have been able to be treated on the spot, and only then if there is an oxygen bed or container to place them in. The only remedy otherwise was and is to come down to lower regions. Next day they took a steamer for Valparaiso which they reached on October 6th. Here they could go on to Brazil either round the Horn or over the mountains. Freathy wanted Francis to go by steamer whilst he went across the mountain but in the end Francis decided to risk the overland way.

Francis wrote, "We went over the Cambra Pass, 13,000 feet, by mule riding, from 2 a.m. till 5 p.m., reaching the railway station on the Argentina side, where we had to wait for 24 hours. The height of the mountains and the length of the journey brought on all the old symptoms. I could not eat, vomited and felt very weak."

Two days on the train brought them to Buenos Aires where they had five days to rest and met Mr. Perugia who had mining interests in the area they proposed to visit. "He told me all about Mr. Carney and of his travels and doings in Brazil and that he was waiting for me to go up and see the diamond district that he thought so favourably of. Mr. Perugia, whilst desirous of having my report, was evidently reluctant to ask me to go on there in my condition. He said it would take 3 weeks and I should have some 100s of miles to travel by mule back. I considered it would be a great pity to go home without having seen these places and I resolved to make the effort and told Mr. Perugia we would go on the next available steamer".

On To the Diamond Trail Again

So off by ship and father and son reached Rio de Janeiro by October 22nd. Here as expected they met Mr. Carney and his son and as soon as Francis could arrange business matters, such as sending word of his next movements to Mr. Pickering, the Secretary to the Kimberley Board and collecting money sent from England they all four set off. There were ten mules including pack mules and there were six guards in their cavalcade. The journey was 24 hours by train and five days by mule to reach Diamantina, the centre of the diamond district where Mr. Carney had been exploring. The long mule back days so exhausted grandfather that whenever there was a stop he had to lie prone. On arrival he rested a day and met several men from the diamond trade.

In part of his report he writes as follows "The diamonds seem to have been discovered from two sources by the diggers, the one alluvial and the other is from the wearing down of the conglomeration of quatzem, sandstone, schist and cemented

Arawatabaru Barima River. British Guiana.

H. K. L. von Zingesar, Georgetown, British Guiana.

Post card sent by Francis Freathy Oats to his cousin Ethel Olds at St Just with the message "the boat in this picture is the same size & build as the one we travelled 400 miles in. F. F. O."

sand and clays, this conglomerate seems to spread over the country for long distances, this country so covered is called Chapada. In the short time at my disposal it would be rash to come to any emphatic conclusion but the conglomerate gave me the impression of being a glacial drift over sandstone, there is evidence enough that it was diamond bearing.....but I have no reason to believe that there was anything eruptive about them." The yield of diamonds from the deposits in the Diamantina district (discovered about a century before this visit) was actually very variable and Brazil was to become a major producer of the gem.

The following week several more mines were visited, one run by a French Company and "I do not think output could cover costs." He continues, "I had a long interview with Mr. Rezandi, an old inhabitant and for many years chief diamond buyer here, and gathered from him that the yield from the conglomerate per 100 cubic metres is extremely low. I also had some conversation with Mr. Humphrey, an American buyer, he has been here 3 years. He is now thinking of bringing in plant to dredge the river. This is a significant fact as he realises this will bring better results than working the surface conglomerate. But he, Mr. Humphrey, thinks that some of the deposits are pipes or craters. I think this is a mistake. All deposits seem to be sedimentary and none eruptive."

The party arrived back in Rio by November 15th and on the 20th boarded a ship for England. Both father and son must have been much looking forward to a happy homecoming in good time to celebrate Christmas in St. Just. For his wife, Elizabeth Ann, the travellers had brought a vicuna skin which she used to keep her warm when she had her daily outing in her carriage. Freathy, too, had a present, from the De Beers company of one hundred pounds, for his 'kind services to his father'.

CHAPTER 8
SOUTH AFRICAN POLITICS

Something of Parliament and Politics and Francis Oats MP in Cape Colony, South Africa

Because Francis Oats was in Parliament at the Cape from 1898 until 1907, I must write something of this time. Politics in this Colony even at an early date were complicated and when Griqualand West was annexed in 1877 doubly so! Until the discovery of diamonds, the Colony was not really felt to be of much value to Great Britain but following that discovery, and of the gold in the Transvaal, more interest was shown, and because of Imperial interest matters often became even more complex. The policies towards her Colonies to alter with new governments in Great Britain caused tensions.

In the earlier days there were not set parties, these formed with the rise of more wealth and more industry, no longer were fruit and wool the only exports. The two opposing parties were the Afrikaaner Bond and Rhodes Imperialistic party and moderate men fell between two stools. After the Jamieson raid, Rhodes fell from power and had to claw his way back through the newly named Progressive party, using bribes: "With the rise of the mining industry expenditure assumed more formidable proportions and corruption increased. The influence of Rhodes increased this trend (bribery in offering blocks of shares, as in the South African Company). Money played an unprecedented role in the general elections of 1898." ('The Founder' page 42 by Rotberg)

This is the year Francis stood for election and he was returned for Namaqualand. Previously John Merriman was the choice, for many years, of the farmers of this sparsely populated area. At this election Rhodes himself came up to canvass votes and make sure the copper miners voted 'Progressive'. Merriman stood successfully for another constituency. But it makes sense of the veiled hostility of Oats and Merriman across the floor of the House, I am sure my grandfather believed in what he stood for, "I am a Britisher", he exclaimed once when asked his politics.

One of his interests lay in the extension of the railways and to have them run as cheaply but as efficiently as possible. Coal for the mines was of paramount importance for the running of mine machinery. Also De Beers had fruit farms and raised horses and cattle and so any schemes for irrigation had his support, water was also needed for the growing population. But what comes through clearly was that he wanted no nonsense and no red tape but that the job should be done competently. One debate of where to site a reservoir was of interest because he thought the expense of a highly qualified expert should be undertaken to make an assessment of the proposed location. There had it seems been failures of such schemes simply because expert advice had not been sought.

There comes too, side by side with the practical man, the thought so often in his mind, for those less fortunate than himself, shown re: the high price of coffee and even in his dislike of policemen in military uniforms, extracts from his speech added below.

Re: Railway Refreshments Contract 1902
"Mr. Oats thought that the charges should be adjusted to meet conditions and requirements of the country better than was the case now. In the case of poor people who had to make long journeys, they had to pay 6d for a cup of coffee which was not worth 1d. (Hear, Hear) That was a crying shame and the House should be no party to such an arrangement, and the case of poor people should be considered so that they could get refreshments at less exorbitant prices."

August 1903 - Re: The Police Force
"Mr. Oats said he wished the Police Force could be reduced:....and that the Force should not dress like the military, especially at such a time as the present. He thought that the men who do the police work should be clothed like policemen when they wished for peace in the country."

In 1904, Francis Oats was the only dissenting vote against the "Chinese Exclusion Bill", proposed to disallow any Chinese, not of British citizenship, to re-enter South Africa after leaving the country. During the debates he was particularly outraged by the claim of Merriman that the Chinese should be kept out, not because of their "vices" but because of their "virtues". He declared that the exclusion of any nationality, on account of its virtues would not have his support. To his mind the Bill was retrogressive and barbaric, and one which could not have been passed if China had a navy like Japan.

In 1908 Francis Oats was offered the chairmanship of the De Beers Company and accepted (ironically, at this time his old political adversary, John Merriman, became Prime Minister). From then on he would be too occupied to be able to attend Parliament and so he stood down. For a great part of his time as a Member, it had been a most difficult period for the country as a whole, his first years lead up to war and then in the aftermath there were the serious matters to be decided upon on the reconstruction of South Africa. By 1908 the time was drawing near to when the country would cease to be a Colony and become a self-governing Dominion – but that is another story.

CHAPTER 9
THE UNBREAKABLE LINK

"They gaze on winding roads
Dear in the ward of memory,
They see the valleyed ways that turn
Down to the sea,
And through the clamour of the stamps
A far off music breaks and swells."

From Homelands by Bernard Moore

The link with his boyhood remained throughout the life of Francis Oats, in his continuing interest and investments in local mines and in the purchase or building of homes for his family in Cornwall. And that he was proud of his heritage is shown in his support for Cornish activities in Kimberley, especially in the New Year's Eve dinners there for One and All. He travelled much on business for his company throughout South Africa and further north. When he went up to Johannesburg his train stopped at Randfontein where often Cornish miners met the train for a chat with Captain Frank and perhaps ask his advice.

He had it seems, mixed with his practical common sense, some of his county's superstitions. He was said to put a small stone inside his pith helmet when he went to areas known for many poisonous snakes. This was supposed to be a deterrent to snake bites!

Before he left on his journey to South America he deposited with his bankers certain instructions including a note to say if he were to die on this trip he would not have done so by suicide. (A cousin in South Africa told me these pieces of 'dark Celtic beliefs' but the latter I certainly do not feel was in this category, until the laws were changed, did not suicide forfeit Christian burial, and even their wills could be suspect.)

Something of the buying and selling of No. 4 Market Street. St. Just

Francis Oats instructed his brother-in-law, Henry Olds by cable to buy the house in 1892 from Mary Harcourt Walker. It came with a garden and six fields (the Lafrowda fields), and some plots of land. The walls about these fields were raised later on, in part to offer work to unemployed miners. Also during the war, Grandfather wrote about the fields to his agent to make sure they were put down to hay to feed cattle at Nanpean, the farm he owned. Also he did try unsuccessfully to exchange them with fields adjoining Nanpean.

In 1909, Francis conveyed the house to Wilfred Oats, "my natural and lawful son,

Photograph of Francis outside Carne House,
No. 4 Market Street, St Just

in consideration of his love and affection for his said son". In 1911, Wilfred Oats, of 7, Hitchfield Terrace, Regents Park, sold Carne House to Peter Olds, butcher, of Trewellard. In 1911, Peter Olds sold it to F. F. Oats. In 1921, Col. F. F. Oats sold it to the Cornwall Territorial Force Association. When the Territorials had the house the Regimental Sergeant (Regular) lived there. Peter Olds bought the Lafrowda fields and also the garden of Carne House. When the house was sold into private ownership, to Mr. and Mrs. Hartley, she told me the only thing lacking about the property was a garden!

Later too, the fields were sold to the council, which built a housing estate and room also for a fire station, library and a group surgery. But the final link was yet to come: over the ensuing years, grandfather was to buy land, and in 1907 to start on the building of a new house for his family using mainly local labour and a St. Just firm of masons.

Back to South Africa

Francis Oats as seen above retained firm ties with Cornwall, but his life work was earned out in South Africa and to this land we will return. Barnato died in 1897, Rhodes was to die in 1902, and Beit in 1906. By 1908 it became Francis Oat's turn in the hot seat – work not death his lot and as Chairman of De Beers his energies were firmly committed. (Did he remember sometimes the start of it all, trudging off as a young lad to Balleswidden? – maybe not – there was far too much involvement in today's battles for him to "day dream").

One and All - December, 1891 - January, 1892

Once a year Cornishmen on the diamond fields of Kimberley got together and had a celebration dinner on the evening of December, 31st. These dinners began in 1890 and were usually held at the Gladstone Hotel. There was a break during the siege of Kimberlev and after the break during the First World War these dinners were not renewed, Captain Quentral and Francis Oats were enthusiastic supporters of this gathering and both died before the War ended. Much good fellowship and jollity was had at the dinners and below are some extracts from the local paper, The Diamond Advertiser, 4th January, 1892.

The large dining room of the hotel was gaily decorated, the old Cornish motto, One and All, conspicuously at the head of the table and Mr. and Mrs. Spargo and their assistants had evidently taken great pain to set the table out to great advantage...

Nor must we forget the dinner committee under the Chairmanship of Captain Quentral, Inspector of Mines and from Wendron did excellent service in bringing about such a successful meeting. They worked indefatigably in securing the attendance of such large numbers of their countrymen, and not only were they able to get several guests from other mines but they succeeded in placing in the Chair on this occasion Captain Francis Oats (St. Just), one of the Directors of the De Beers Company, himself a brother Cornishman and who won the hearts of all by his warm-hearted geniality and bon hommie.

Mr. McHardy, Manager of Kimberley Mine was the guest of honour. His speech had much praise for Cornish miners in the diamond fields and Francis Oats, in replying, thanked him and "he would not add more lest he should make them blush!" He continued "such remarks came well from one who had so much to do with Cornishmen on the fields and who in all his dealings with them had exhibited no favouritism. As time went on the occupation of the miner became of more and more importance all over the world, they were really and truly the men of the soil and as in these times the dignity of labour was universally acknowledged, so they found that the labour of the mine was infinitely more appreciated than it was in times past. And so they also found that the men whose hands were horny by hard labour in a mine, as well as the men who were placed in a superior position, were able to discharge their respective duties with the pluck, energy and perseverance that Mr. McHardy had talked about and which he (the Chairman) could endorse from many years experience. As they all knew, mines in Kimberley were of a peculiar and distinct character, and to some extent, when they first came out, miners found themselves somewhat at sea but by the use of their intelligence and experience they had acquired at Home, they very soon overcame all difficulties and he hoped that in time they would all turn out useful men. (Cheers)"

Captain Quentral made a speech and complemented the Chairman. He then proposed the toast "Success to the Mining Industry and the trade of the Diamond Fields" and the Chairman, responding, said they would perhaps excuse him if he spoke to his people in their own language and then proceeded to speak in the Cornish dialect in happy terms to the infinite delight of all the Cornishmen present, at the same time he glanced slyly at the reporters who were of course quite unable to follow him.

One year there was a great feeling of dissatisfaction and disappointment; perhaps their dinner was held at a strange venue? For there was not a pasty in sight, nor a bowl of cream!!

How Traditions are Kept

One day in Johannesburg about the turn of the century grandfather, Francis Oats was descending a mine in a skip or gig. Two other men were going down too. The skip rocketed downward and the two men in a panic, prepared to jump off, as they thought it was out of control. Grandfather had no time to do more than seize the fellows by the collars of their jackets and restrain them and the skip came to rest at one of the mine levels. He knew the skip used to go very fast, the men could have been badly injured. In the Cornish mines there could be nasty accidents, a miner's foot had only to miss a ladder rung, or his boot slip in a wet place. Must have been second nature to Francis to think quickly and not waste a moment. (I know of the above from my elder brother who was told it by our father long ago).

A Farming Streak?

When Francis Oats began buying land, largely from Lord Falmouth, from the mid 1890s around and about Cape Cornwall, he must have had in his mind more building and buying. And I think maybe, it was his interest in the South African fruit farms made him build early on two large greenhouses, one above Priest's Cove and the second on the driveway of Nanpean Farm. Long before his new home was built his family had from these greenhouses plenty of fruit and once in their prime, the wonder gardener Leah could send up grapes, peaches, nectarines etc., so that visitors, many from South Africa, might imagine themselves in hotter climes, and even forget a thick blanket of fog!

Then Nanpean, the farm not a farm as he wrote, gave him much satisfaction. "My son and I are anxious to build it up". It was in a very run down state and was covered mainly with mine diggings both very old and less so, but now non-productive, or at least with the low prices for tin. So with Freathy running the place in his absence they had it cleared of stones, ditches filled in and hedges rebuilt and a great retaining wall to contain sloping fields beside a hard track way. The old adit on the farm was turned into a series of gardens, not in the same category as the hanging gardens of Babylon! But none the less very pleasing sheltered places. Great granite steps let into the high walls leading from the highest garden near Nanpean farm to the lowest running down towards the sea. I can remember these gardens well, and Mr. and Mrs. Leah and with my sister enjoyed playing with their daughter, Ancey. Mr. Leah was a farmer's son but from where in Cornwall I do not know.

When Francis was home in Cornwall, ways and means of improving the farm after its years of neglect were deeply discussed with his son and the bailiff. The First World War brought many problems with his son away in the forces and other workers gone too. There was a bad period when no woman could be found to do the dairy work, women too, gone to help in the war effort.

From Africa he continued to give the little farm his thoughts and the letters back to Cornwall bear witness to this. What acreage was laid down to hay? How much stock was being carried? I feel it was an outlet from his every day running of the company with all the increased problems brought about during wartime everywhere, and as gardening is a solace to so many of us, so the little farm held his attention.

And was it not natural, even for so practical a man, that he should retain links from his forebears? His grandfather, although a tinner at his marriage, saved enough to buy a small-holding and his father in middle life came to farm at South Torfrey. The working miner often had some land on which he worked when not at the mine, if only a plot for potatoes or to keep a pig. It gave the feeling of growing things in the open air but above all it added to the small income a miner earned. Francis was only six when they left Golant to settle in St. Just but he would have distinct memories of his earliest years as we all have of our first environments.

When he first went out to South Africa, life was all taken up with mining and attendant problems; farming and mining there were quite separate, no possibility of doing much in the Kimberley dust. Produce was brought into the town from miles around. Later on it was, when he was settled and growing wealthier, that he had time for touring the fruit farms and interesting himself more deeply in the company's farms and stock around Kimberley. In Cornwall there were six fields to Carne House and then Nanpean the farm not a farm when he bought it, kept a place in his mind ever after.

CHAPTER 10
THE GREAT DIAMOND HOAX

The Lemoine Affair, in which Francis Oats had a part to play

This case made headlines between 1905 and 1908 and I became interested in it because, eventually, Francis Oats was drawn in. The more I delved into *The Times* newspaper of those dates, the more intrigued I became. Henri Lemoine was being investigated for fraud, claiming to make artificial diamonds, and the investigations dragged on over years. Public interest was kept awake over long periods and the matter was much discussed. In those Edwardian days every woman it seemed dreamed of these gems! And not only women, the male adorned himself in winking tie-pins, cufflinks and so on, Much of the story eventually unfolded and seems, at least from this distance, both dramatic and hilarious. Even the young budding writer, Proust, was to use the case, describing it in different ways as it might have been recounted by Flaubert, Saint Beuve, Balzac etc..

Earlier in the century, M. Henri Moissan, the French physicist and Nobel Prize winner, had reported that he had manufactured diamonds. The diamonds were perfect but tiny and cost so much to make that as a business they could never rival natural diamonds. Earlier still, J. B. Hannay had likewise produced diamonds, and there the matter ended.

But did it? For in 1905, an electrical engineer, once employed by M. Moissan, announced he had perfected a new formula and that he could produce large diamonds. His name was Henri Lemoine, he had an engaging personality and was well able to make his invention sound plausible. Some British industrialists became interested and hey presto! in no time at all he had an introduction to one of the world's richest men, Sir Julius Wernher, a partner to Alfred Beit and life governor of De Beers; he demonstrated before them and produced flawless diamonds. Both partners were convinced and Wernher agreed to pay Lemoine a large sum of money to set up a factory in the Pyrenees to continue his experiments and all was to be kept secret. The formula for the making of these diamonds, unseen by Wernher was lodged in a London bank and not to be disclosed unless they agreed. The De Beers company feared that unless such an invention were brought under control it would wreck the diamond industry. Even the mere rumour of its existence could cause a selling panic among the investors in De Beers.

Time went by. Lemoine demanded more money; he had already received about £64,000! Beit was dead. Wernher became worried and decided to speak to Dr. Jamieson, approaching the end of his term as Prime Minister of the Cape Colony, who took a very serious view of the matter. Didn't the diamond mines bring wealth to the country? He contacted Francis Oats, both a fellow director of De Beers and a friend of early Kimberley days. It was arranged the latter should go secretly to

Paris.

There seem varied reports as to what transpired in the Paris cellar. Chivers in his story of De Beers makes no mention of the problem at all, how be it some of the Company's Directors were involved! Neither is it mentioned in the annals of De Beers by Gardiner Williams, I suppose not his special sphere. Both Brian Roberts in "the Diamond Magnates' and Geoffrey Wheatcliff in 'The Randlords', fill in the story well. Also at the time of the trial both 'The Mining World' and 'The Mining Journal' made reports. But sufficient here to quote from the Standard Encyclopaedia of South Africa Vol. III. "Francis Oats, more sceptical than Wernher, decided to visit France and examine Lemoine's diamonds for himself. He immediately noticed their resemblance to Kimberley stones and was convinced there was fraud."

The electric furnace was in the basement of a warehouse. The heat, the little window, the dark spaces, what an ideal setting for tricks, even if the presenter held the stage clad in his birthday suit, so he could not be accused of hiding anything! What ever happened that day the trickster had met his match!! Francis Oats watched very keenly.

Afterwards he said the furnace was a 'nonsense', a word he used often whilst sitting in the Cape Parliament and that the diamonds produced were perfect Kimberley stones! (which indeed they were, Lemoine used to buy from jewellers to help him make an artificial diamond). Francis said Lemoine was an impostor, then he returned to South Africa. Wernher was forced to prosecute and the trial continued for months. Wernher, and the gullibility of this wealthy gentleman, sent Parisians into great mirth. Fraudulent Lemoine was proved by and by but he was a most engaging rogue and Paris applauded!

He was let out on bail by the Magistrate in charge of the case, to assemble material and crucibles for another public demonstration to prove his innocence. He was at large for two months and kept this magistrate, M. Le Poittevin, satisfied with one excuse after another for the delay. Finally he was told to appear on June 17th when Wernher too would be present.

And so the charade continues. Lemoine, being a fraud and about to be found out, what would he do? Escape, of course, but oh, so carefully and well planned. Two days before the 17th, he quietly leaves his house in a respectable suburb, he goes on foot, the tell-tale car remains before the house, he cannot be far! He disappears. Sometime later in the evening a cab carries away his family and lastly a truck load of household goods leaves and vanishes too! Subsequently it comes to light that for these last two months the family were selling valuables and preparing to flit!

June 17th arrives and the accusers, Wernher, Fieldenheim, and their witnesses and lawyers assemble outside the magistrates chambers. Was it a little stuffy? Was the magistrate a little late? Did the gentlemen in their formal clothes with barbered heads and beards grow irritable? At last the door opens and M. Le Poittevin stands there. Ah, non, Messieurs, he will not come, he went away on Monday there is a warrant for his arrest!

They gather in the office and now the packet with the formula is to be opened, it is removed from its outer wrapping, there are five seals. At last these are broken. The

Magistrate reads:

Take Carbon. Crystallise it and submit it to the necessary pressure. You will have diamonds.

Oh, what a joke, what! Stiff pages with but a school boy's instructions. All are thunderstruck! It is ridiculous! Someone present exclaims, "C'est une joyeuse fumistie!" and with this merry quip we can leave this time more or less, not a great deal to tell. Lemoine is sentenced in his absence to ten years imprisonment. Wernher and Fieldenhelm get some compensation. The Chamber of the Syndicate and the diamond merchants receive a shilling!

Really the only sad figure in the case seems the plausible M. Le Poittevin who was suspended from office for his handling of this case. Lemoine and his family are comfortably in Constantinople. However, a few years later he returns to France thinking the scandal had died down, only to have the police officers knocking on his door. Lemoine insists they come in to enjoy a glass of wine before arresting him and to enable himself and family to finish their supper!

CHAPTER 11
MORE ST. JUST MATTERS

Some Family Matters Concerning the Building of a new Home and a Wedding

My First Visit to St. Just, by Dorothy Brown in 1907

I was met off the Cornish Riviera Express at 5 p.m. by Elise and her mother ('Madam' as my family always called her), who was to be my future mother-in-law. We drove out in the then well-known chaise driven by an old man called Hall in a bowler hat, carriage rather low and like an open Victoria (two sat back to back to the horse, one and the driver opposite where the only view was of the horses buttocks. The reins were put through a sort of loop in the shape of a question mark).

The long climb up out of Penzance and Newbridge to the moorland and Bostraze bog overlooking the hideous china clay settling pits, mist sweeping from the south west, an altogether dismal view. Had I not the thought of Freathy, who by then was on his way back from Freiberg, Saxony, I could have turned back there and then.

All was cheerful, however, on arrival at Carne House at the end of Market Street. Three sisters (maids) welcomed us. Elise did the main cooking and excellent it was too. Giles came down later with two girls he'd met on board ship. They were fun. We used to go to the Cape nearly everyday, bathing and for picnics and some days for long walks to the moors or along the cliff path to Sennen or to Pendeen Manor for teas and so on, sometimes to Penzance to see a bioscope, the forerunner of the cinema. The motor buses had not arrived in those days, the local service then consisted of a horse drawn bus, open-top with two horses and a driver called Thomas Archelaus.

Porthledden was at the foundation stage and the upper and lower Praze houses then being added to the older Middle Praze where Mr. and Mrs. Leah, the gardener lived, not only a gardener and agent on the property when Freathy was in Germany, but first and foremost a friend of the family. The greenhouses at the farm, Nanpean, and the ones at the Cape were already built and peaches and nectarines, grapes and tomatoes all grow there, also early potatoes.

Freathy arrived home soon for a few weeks leave to see how Porthledden was progressing. He used to take out lunch to the empty new Lower Praze and spend most of the day around the place. I think the farmhouse was built then and occupied by a Bailiff. In those days there were over one hundred pigs, a pedigree herd of cows and the bull, Guernseys, no sheep, and the usual poultry of those days, grey Plymouth Rocks, besides peahens, which belonged to Madam, and six horses about the farm.

Freathy had a small two-seater car, a Singer. You sat high above the road, were exceeding the speed limit at forty miles an hour, the car had all its 'entrails visible'! Still, we had some wonderful outings together in it. It was the second car registered in Cornwall, numbered A F 2."

Something of the building of Porthledden to be a home for the Oats Family 1907 - 1909

Francis Oats had been buying land during the preceding years from the turn of the century. His brother-in-law, Henry Olds sometimes acted for him if he was in South Africa. Most of the land belonged to Lord Falmouth and some to Lord Clifton. The very last purchase was towards the end of World War 1. In a letter to him his son, Freathy mentions 14 acres and a small house and out-buildings. This was Lower Boswedden, and the fields run down towards Kenidjack Valley and "abutted the Nanpean border there". There were recently closed mines down on the cliffs and hillsides with their attendant buildings and waste tips.

Porthledden under construction.

Before a start was made on the house, greenhouses were built, some on the south below the Cape above Priests Cove and others alongside the drive into the farm. Produce from these supplied the family whilst still at Carne House. Next were built two houses, one on either side of the original cottage, these were the Praze houses, which made a small row, just above the entrance gates into Porthledden. Praze means a meadow. In the middle one lived Mr. and Mrs. Leah. He managed the greenhouses and in due course would be in charge of the laying out of the gardens. Mrs. Leah came from London. I can remember them well with their daughter, Ancey, who was a little older. During the war years Mr. Leah, it was who kept things going, trustworthy in all things and to my parents, a true friend.

Everything seems to have preceded the building of Porthledden. On the farm was the small farm cottage and this was left in situ but a much larger and modern farmhouse was erected on the seaward side with a large cool dairy adjoining the house. Following on, fine new farm buildings went up, far better than any in the area at this time, running water in the cow-barn, the stables had a carpenter's shop built above, and on the opposite side of the yard a long row of good pig sties built with inner sleeping quarters and a little courtyard run adjoining.

New hen-houses were built south of the farmhouse. I remember this farm with every kind of animal, save sheep, which did not thrive here, even to guinea-fowl chittering about. The original ones belonged to Elizabeth Ann, doubtless brought across from South Africa and with mention of this land, tell too, of the two meerkats kept as pets at Porthledden, I have seen photographs of them. My mother said they were engaging little creatures and that somehow one was drowned in the cove.

Returning to the new hen-house, below it was a flat piece of ground, as I remember it, used for the hens to wander in. But, surprise, surprise, earlier the Oats and their friends had made use of it as a tennis court. There are some priceless photos of this time, ladies in summery long dresses, men lounging about! Picnic things spread about and in one an odd looking pram and a frilly-bonneted baby looking out!

Below this little plat the ground dropped steeply away, part of the old mine-workings. These were put to fine use, turned into deep sheltered gardens on several levels. Tall granite walls protected them and down the sides of these walls protruded steps, just room for your foot and no handrails which led from one level to another. The lowest level was hundreds of feet below and out of it led a door into the field above Cove Cottage. This place was called the Quillets (quillet means enclosure). Here were grown early potatoes and other early vegetables, strawberries, sweet violets, apples espaliered against the walls ....it was like no garden I have seen since although by the time I came to explore here, it had been left to grow wild, a secret garden all of my own.

The farm was kept by the family with a bailiff and so it was of great interest to them, from the herd of pedigree pigs, who in summer time were allowed to root about in the near field, to the produce of the dairy with the rich creamy milk of the Guernsey herd and the fresh eggs they could collect warm from the nests. Six horses were kept, but these included a riding horse for my mother and two carriage horses for Madam (Elizabeth Ann) mainly. My father used one of the latter horses if he rode with my mother on occasions. So it would seem the farm was worked by three horses.

In the driveway on the farm-side of the greenhouses, a garage for several cars was built which included a little office equipped with a telephone. Across from here on the edge of fields loomed the burly stone-built water tank which not only supplied water pumped up from the leat in Kenidjack Valley almost on the shore, to Porthledden, the farm, water troughs in the fields, the cottages, but to the town of St. Just also. In the driveway were planted shrubs, some strange ones too, from New Zealand which only flowered every seven years!! At the entrance a heavy gate painted white and in the wall beside, the post box was fixed. And now the turn of the house.

The story is told by our family that one day Francis was plonked unceremoniously

One of the Porthledden meerkats.

atop the highest hedge about place. In Cornwall a hedge generally meant a wall built of rough-hewn stones with an earth 'core' – the earth between the stones ensures a 'living' wall. Giles, his youngest son, and his daughter Elise, abetting, had hoisted him up there and threatened to leave him there if he would not agree to build the home. Well, not where he had planned, which was about where the new farmhouse now stands, but to the north of the farm on the highest piece of land, literally on the hill above the Cape, so that later from the great bow-window on the half-way landing, one looks directly to the stack atop the Cape and to the sea stretching on either side, Porthledden to the north and Priests Cove to the south and beyond only Atlantic breakers, the Isles of Scilly faint on the horizon (but not so if rain was threatening) and then only sea and sky towards America.

Back to my grandfather perched up high. Francis Oats was a short man and by this time middle aged and stoutish, probably inclined to breathlessness! So he succumbed and was lifted down doubtlessly with laughter and Porthledden is on the hill-top!

It rose, not grandly, but firm and sure, built of that pleasing soft-brown granite known as 'white granite' and in it mica winked at you even on the greyest day. The roof slates were green, which mother said came from Cumbria though there were green slates quarried then at Penberthy. The builder of the house was Penrose Marks of St. Just and the only men who worked here who were not local were Italians who came to lay terrazzo flooring in bathrooms (how cold to bare feet!), cloakrooms, kitchen, larders and all the corridors leading to these rooms.

There remains no plan of the building and of course, such bodies as planning authorities did not exist then. Via mother comes the story that grandfather on his travels, once saw a manor house in Somerset with some features he had incorporated into Porthledden including rooms surrounding a courtyard.

Anyway it was surely built, not ornate and the windows, even on the north side were broad and lit with maximum amounts of light, the loveliest window, the bay one on the half-landing. Here one could sit in the window seat, especially at sunset time and gaze at the splendour of shining water alight with brilliant tints from the sinking sun, till the final green flash. The panes were leaded and fitted by Crittals, still in business as I used them for my own home in about 1978.

On the third floor was built a little balcony jutting out far above the wide front doorway and a flag-staff fitted there. On national days of celebration here flew the Union Jack and on local days of note and oh proud honour! on the birthdays of sons and daughters born here. Before sundown the flag was struck.

The new home was called simply Porthledden, taking its name from the bay north of the Cape. Odd persons now and again added 'House' to it, but this was never used by our family. It was in the spring of 1909 they moved in. The boiler house was being fitted with the furnace to heat the water and warm the radiators. Only the conservatory on the east side of the house, beyond the billiard room was still to be completed.

An onlooker watching the place being built, said to grandfather "Why so big?", "Oh, may do as a hotel one day", he replied!

Making the Garden

In this exposed place open to all the Atlantic gales, nothing grew taller than a thorn bush and a few scraggy sycamores and much furze under which the rabbits burrowed. To make a garden here needed much thought. Without shelter nothing could be expected to thrive. So hedges were planted up the driveway and around the lawns being laid down. On one side of the drive, I remember a sturdy hedge of the lovely common fuchsia and on the opposite side alongside a little copse of bent sycamores, a hedge of escallonias grew tall and thick, hiding and at the same time sheltering a little path through the copse and when the winds blew, this was like a sheltered tunnel bringing one out by the gates below the Praze. In the area set aside for vegetables and fruit trees, little quillets were designed, each one with hedges on all sides and an opening or arch in the hedge as an entrance from one to the other and to the main hard-core path which ran along under the high stone walls. Some of the stone for the walls was taken from a little quarry below the engine house outside a gateway in the north wall. Hundreds of feet of sacking were used to protect the little shrubs during their early growth as is carried out on the Isles of Scilly.

Part of the interior of Porhtledden.

The boundary walls, 12 feet tall, were built by unemployed miners and the plain stone covered with lime and plaster, but elsewhere containing walls were lower and built of dressed granite blocks. These same miners were employed for a good time clearing buildings from the several mines once in production there and using the stone to build walls round the quillets and a high retaining wall round a steep field which overhung the pathway up to the two Bounds cottages on the cliffs. Many of the mine dumps were levelled, fine granite stiles built and seats set into some of the walls so that cliff walkers could pause to rest and enjoy the views

Back inside the garden vegetables were sown, plenty of good Cornish potatoes, both early and late, and fruit trees manured and pruned and gradually every plant grew to maturity so that by the time my sister and myself arrived the garden was full of delights.

Mother had a little sunken garden, the sundial there fixed inside an old millstone central hole, and here in this garden grew the old fashioned sweetly scented roses. Ruth, my sister and myself were even made a little sunken place of our own under the tennis lawn where little paths were made to wind about, the small beds bounded by rounded beach stones and grey gritty sand on the paths. Down from the yard gate to the north gate onto the cliffs and the engine house, grew a privet hedge which had reached a huge height by this time. In the summer the heavy scented flowers grew thick and were surrounded by crowds of peacock and red admiral butterflies. Alongside in a little copse, had been laid a rough stone path and on each side in spring the ground was completely covered with primroses, from the creamy soft-eyed flowers their gentle scent filled the air.

Part of the interior of Porthledden.

Down on the seaward slopes of the garden beyond the sloping lawns the gorse had been, in the main, ousted by plantings of the common veronica called Blue Gem by nurserymen I think, but the rabbits remained still in scores. Just off one of the intersecting paths through these bushes was a sunken area and horrible smells sometimes wafted up. Years later when I returned from South Africa and my own children wandered Porthledden, sadly at that time empty, we came to this 'hidden rockery', down some steps. A wonderful sheltered area. And no longer any smells! Recounting this to my brother, John Freathy, a little later, he laughed. "Didn't you know it was the sewage outlet for the house which seeped into an adit in the cliffs?" The rockery had been built to try to hide it from view. Long before our rediscovery, mains sewage had been installed and the rockery was just an area of overgrown shrubs and ericas and the steps shrouded under veronica branches, giving the place its secret air.

Forgive me wandering in the garden of my childhood with such delight. At the time I write this, the place is deserted more or less and no longer owned by our family. When I go to St. Just I cannot bear to go near, only seeing the dear long-lost home from cliffs to the north or from Carn Gloose.

Better to speak of the days up to the Great War and the family entertaining. When Francis Oats came back for a few months from Kimberley, my parents used to be extra busy entertaining business colleagues and friends, a good few from South Africa. Mr. Hirshorn, a fellow director was a welcome visitor. The young Ernest Oppenheimer was a guest several times and from France used to come the whole family; Chaplet, the father, was manager of the asbestos factory at Lavat in Normandy. The latter and Francis Oats met over business one summer in France and he had some of his own family with him, including Dorothy, his daughter-in-law. They all became firm friends. (Of course, in those days asbestos was the new wonder discovery and Francis Oats helped market it. Then nothing was suspected of its lethal qualities.)

Another visitor was Sir Thomas Lipton (owner of one of the first 'chain' stores). He had his yacht, the Shamrock, moored off Priests Cove, it was built as a challenger in the Americas Cup race. If one had asked more and listened more, perhaps one would remember the mention of more individuals. As it is, even so late in my life, I am in correspondence with an erstwhile visitor. Her father was English, her mother American and were living in Dresden when my mother went to 'finish' there after her school days. Francis Freathy was studying in Freiberg also. All these parties met and became lifelong friends. My mother was corresponding up to her death and I have continued to keep the link. The family is called Young and it is to Dorothy I write. She has sent me a photo taken on Porthledden steps, the very first Christmas

Porthledden completed with Cape Cornwall in the background.

70

time in 1909 with herself as a young girl, eight maybe, also a sister, parents very fashionably dressed and Elise Oats and Madam, neither very dressy! Plenty of shawls and woollen hats to keep out the wind, Madam superbly indifferent, with a scarf swathed over a velour hat and tied under a rather fat chin! Dorothy remembers those early days at Porthledden....and no shadow of the frightful war on the horizon. She writes, 'It was a merry household'.

Francis Freathy and Dorothy Brown

In 1907, my mother, Dorothy Brown came for the first time to St. Just. Her first-hand description and her stay in Carne House are too excellent not to include here. She was to marry Francis Freathy Oats in 1909. She and Elise Oats were school fellows at Wyckham Abbey School and it was when Francis Freathy was on a visit to his sister there that he and Dorothy first met.

They were married in the Parish Church at Bletchingley where the Brown family had a tall ivy-clad house on the outskirts of the village. The bride's father was head of a firm of solicitors practising in London, which firm his father had founded. But this is two years too soon. Much was to follow on the 1907 visit of Dorothy's. Following upon it Dorothy and Elise were to be allowed to share rooms together in a pension in Dresden, Elise was very musical and Dorothy was to learn German. Of course, Freathy was not so far off attending to or attempting to, his studies at the Mining School in Freiberg. During the six months his sister and Dorothy were here, the latter and Freathy became engaged with the blessing of both families. Francis Oats told his son he would have to qualify before he would permit him to marry, a good spur and in any case he held all the purse strings!

In the following months Freathy was to visit Highfields, his fiancée's home and in the early summer of 1909, John and Laura Brown, her parents, went down to stay with the Oats family whilst Francis was at Porthledden.

In October, the families assembled for the wedding to be held on the 6th of the month. Everybody was present, except for Jessie, the eldest Brown daughter, who had settled the previous year in Canada. At Highfields, Madam had her own bedroom and sitting room and her own maid whilst staying there. Also a carriage and pair were put at her disposal. It was quite a big village wedding, and there is a description elsewhere of the bride and groom and 'priceless' pre-wedding studio photos. Also of the guests and clothes and the wedding breakfast laid out in a huge marquee on the Highfields lawns and something of her wedding day reminiscences written for us many years later by our mother.

Only one story here, which is personal to myself. In 1972, I went out to British Columbia to stay with my aunt Jessie Brown. When she had finished her training at Slade School of Art she visited Canada, accompanying friends and on returning, asked her parents permission to emigrate. There she became an art teacher. She was a wonderful woman, now, 90 years old, and still taking some lessons in her studio and arranging exhibitions.

Whilst we were sitting together one day, she took something from a little drawer and laid it on my lap....three pairs of gloves....beautiful they were and in good condition. These she told me were the three remaining pairs of the six she had

71

received from Paris in 1909. They were a present from her sister's father-in-law. She was the only relative not present at her sister's wedding or at the reception in her old home and he remembered her. Across the years, I knew from her voice, with what joy she had received this token. It was not the fineness of the gloves each pair was for a different occasion and of a variety of materials and the artist would know the beautiful workmanship therein. No, it was the sweet thought that prompted the gift. It gave a soft glow to her face and I too remember it across the years.

After the marriage, and when Francis Oats was about to return to Africa, he wrote to his daughter-in-law wishing her and Freathy happiness. His handwriting was about as illegible as I am told mine is! One could unravel some sentences from this letter with its thin spidery strokes. He told her he was sure she should prove a loyal helpmate to his son and said he had not thought Freathy would have had such sense to choose so suitable a wife!

It is Dorothy, my mother's affection for her father-in-law and her stories of his kindness and his entertaining personality which give me intense interest and involvement in Francis Oats. Across the years a warmth comes down to me.

Dinner at the Cape, November 1909 (From a Newspaper Account)

On the occasion of the return of Mr. and Mrs. F. F. Oats from their honeymoon, invitations were issued to all employees and tenants with their wives and families, numbering 130 to Cape Cornwall Refreshment Rooms. A sumptuous dinner was provided consisting of roast and boiled beef, pork, mutton and lamb, meat pies and fruits of all kinds. Mr. Olds presided. After the tables had been cleared, Mr. Olds proposed the usual loyal toasts. Then came the toast of the evening, 'Mr. and Mrs. F. F. Oats', proposed by Mr. Crang, who remarked that he felt sure he was correct in saying that all the employees were highly pleased in the choice Mr. Oats had made in regard to his wife, (loud cheers). She was welcomed at Porthledden in no small degree, and he was sure what was the Parish of Bletchingley's loss was St. Just's gain and also Mrs. Oats was a lady they would all be proud to welcome, (loud applause).

Mr. Holman said he quite endorsed Mr. Crang's remarks in every respect. About ten years ago he underwent the same responsibility Mr. Oats had, and he hoped they would have the same happiness he had had.

Mr. Oats in replying said he did not know whether it was he who chose his wife, or his wife had chosen him but, at any rate they were got together and he was pleased to see such a jolly gathering. He said he really did not know that the employees of Porthledden were so many, including their families, as there were that night and he hoped that as the little mines were developing, more would be employed.

The next toast was 'Mr. and Mrs. Francis Oats and family'. Mr. P. H. Roberts said he had known Mr. Frank Oats from a boy. Many had left St. Just for foreign shores, but none had done better than Mr. Oats. He was a good employer and a good master. Mr. Marks said he never wished to work for a

72

better master, as regards Mrs. Oats, he had known her all his lifetime and she was a lady who always tried to do good to her neighbours.

Mr. Leah said he had worked for Mr. Oats for seven years and was proud to work for such a master. He was able to say that the improvements Mr. Oats was making on the estate were the means of providing work for a large number of hands. No one could estimate the money that had been laid out and the workmen benefited by it.

The toast of Miss Elise Oats was drunk next and Mr. Crang said that all the praise for decorating the tables etc.. was due to Miss Oats. She had worked hard and was the means of making the evening a complete success. The last toast of the evening was then drunk. This was 'Miss Pyle and the servants'. Mr. Crang said that all who were here this evening were indebted to Miss Pyle for the part she had taken. As regards the servants, they had all helped splendidly which meant success. The toast was drunk with enthusiasm!

All the company acknowledged that they had spent a most happy and enjoyable evening and ringing cheers were given for Mr. and Mrs. F. F. Oats and they were wished much happiness in their new sphere of life. As only persons of 12 years and over were invited, Mrs. Oats, Senior, presented for all those under that age, a box of chocolates.

After the dinner was over, Mr. Oats invited all the employees to Porthledden to inspect the numerous wedding presents. The following additional presents were received by the couple that were not in the list published last week.

Barometer by the Levant Staff
Silver Salver by the Basset Staff
Two Silver Fruit Spoons by Doctor and Mrs. Nesbitt
Two Silver Serviette Rings by Mr. and Mrs. W. T. Williams

The Oats family had been settled in Porthledden since the spring, probably about the time Francis Oats came over from South Africa and only the conservatory was still to be built on the east of the billiard room. Elizabeth Ann had the south-east and the south room. My mother said she was very fond of her. She was a partial invalid from a stroke years before, but full of fun. She had her own maid, Lizzie Williams, who accompanied her too, on overseas journeys. And at Porthledden she had a carriage and pair and drove out every afternoon, wet or fine!

After their honeymoon, Freathy and Dorothy settled in and my mother said she was always mistress of Porthledden. In the last weeks of the year, Elise left with her mother for the Cape to become engaged to Robert Leith, a doctor practising in Port Elizabeth. They both came back again prior to the wedding which was held in Africa and left some time later in 1910.

CHAPTER 12
CHAIRMAN OATS

Mainly Diamond Matters

'Men with strong personalities spoke from the Chair'
'FRANCIS OATS ...... self made, able, entertaining, energetic'
Quotes above from *The Story of De Beers* by Chivers

When Francis Oats was voted the chairman of De Beers Consolidated Diamond Mines Company Ltd. in 1908 he had ceased to be a Member of Parliament. He now was in a position of responsibility and power and, with his board to help him, had the heavy task of running the huge De Beers concerns. I do not intend to go deeply into his work because this is only a brief account of his life and not being an expert in any field, I cannot comment with any authority on such matters. I will include extracts from some of the speeches at the Annual General Meetings so that the varied matters dealt with can be seen and, of course, all are preserved in the Company's archives in Kimberley.

The early part of his chairmanship was difficult for Francis. After Rhodes' death, the management of De Beers had based its monopoly on the proposition that there would be no new major discoveries of diamonds. When a bricklayer named Thomas M. Cullinan claimed to have discovered diamonds in a huge oval of yellow dirt some 600 miles north of Kimberley, De Beers geologists scoffed at the idea of diamond pipes existing outside of the Kimberley area. Francis had declared that "the whole thing was a fake". He suggested to De Beers stockholders that the mine, which Cullinan named the Premier Mine, had been "salted" with diamonds from the Kimberley area.

It quickly turned out that Francis had been wrong. The Premier was a diamond pipe, larger than any other found in the world and four times the size of Kimberley's Big Hole mine. When the news was conveyed to Alfred Beit, who along with Rhodes and Barnato been a life governor of De Beers, he had a heart attack from which he never recovered.

Cullinan himself was prepared to fight another diamond war rather than sell out to De Beers. To raise capital for this mine, he sold a majority interest to the Transvaal government. Fortunately for De Beers, the British had just triumphed over the Boer settlers in the Transvaal in the Anglo-Boer War, and they were able to pressure the Transvaal into coming to terms with De Beers.

When I was in Kimberley, in 1989, I was shown a film about the De Beers company and I noted how Rhodes was central and when he was gone it was all Ernest Oppenheimer. The two men who followed Rhodes were not mentioned. Maybe I'm over-sensitive! The first man, Sir Lewis Michell had an unenviable task following on

Horse-play on the long steamer journey.

from the founder of the firm and Francis Oats had an equally unpleasant beginning, having to cope during the world recession and when he had guided the Company to better times, all too soon came the problems brought about by the First World War.

In Kimberley the Oats had a family house in Belgravia. I now know when this home was given up possibly after Porthledden was complete and about the time of Francis's daughter's marriage. Sometime in this period he arranged to rent a little bungalow owned by De Beers. A quite humble looking establishment which is still in situ, No. 15 Park Lane. It is still typical of such places, a corrugated iron roof with a veranda around the building. I saw it myself, the little garden rather overgrown and even still an ancient looking rain tank. It would have been a place quite sufficient for Francis' needs at this point in his life, with his wife often in Cornwall and when in Africa, down in Port Elizabeth at their daughter's home. At the bungalow there would be a servant to care for him and he was often away. Then if he wished to entertain he could do so at the very comfortable Club nearer the centre of the City.

After the two weddings, the next excitement was naturally the arrival of the first grandchild, in Cornwall, with a second due soon at Bird Street, Port Elizabeth. In 1912, the proud parents came on a visit from Cornwall bringing the new Francis Edwin. I think, perhaps, that Elizabeth Ann travelled with them, to be with her daughter. On board ship some scenes are still there on the old brown photos, deck chairs with reclining ladies, a baby with a frilly bonnet and some with his mother cradling him and others with the white clad nurse. There are other faded, priceless scenes of deck quoits and one with 'Papa' in flannels astride the slippery pole trying to unseat his adversary!

On arrival in Cape Town, they boarded the White Train for the north being privileged to occupy the De Beers coach, which was equipped with every luxury. This train carriage was specially made in America and is now in the mine museum in Kimberley. Even today its opulence is very evident from the mahogany furnishings and plush upholstered seating to the table laid for dinner with gleaming silver and crystal cut glass. Rhodes may have roughed it in Rhodesia and in Kimberley slept on an iron truckle bed but if he wished to impress his visitors or guests he did not spare money.

Family group on a steamer to South Africa in 1912.

Only a little comes down of the nine months the little family spent in Africa this year. When they stayed in Kimberley their base was at the Belgrave Hotel, which had in the first instance been built in fine style for Rhodes as a sanatorium. Rhodes hoped it would attract rich invalids needing the bracing air of this high plateau, but in this instance his business sense did not pay off because the climate, pleasant at times, could also reach extremes of heat and cold, with rain and dust storms. So, here stayed Dorothy, baby, nanny and Freathy too in between much travelling about with his father on a round of De Beers interests and properties. I am sure Dorothy was taken to see places too. The lovely fruit farms of the Cape and down to stay in Bird Street, the home of her friend and relation now, and Bob Leith her husband.

Apart from the photos of the days at sea and the odd glimpses told me by my mother, there are two concrete mementos of this time in my possession. These are two old post cards sent to Dorothy by her husband and they come from South West Africa and dated November 2nd and December 28th, 1912.

Francis Oats had come up to South West Africa, accompanied by his son Freathy, to visit the German colony and see their diamond extraction in progress. On this coast the dunes were found to be more or less littered with the gemstones. There were also large finds at the mouth of the Orange River and with the policy of his company to control the sale of diamonds, so that the market did not become glutted and prices fall, it was important to see the extent of these diggings and to make agreements for the sale of diamonds to counteract a surfeit on the market. He found the diamonds produced inferior to the Kimberley ones and thus perhaps hoped they would not affect the sales for De Beers.

They stopped at the whaling station as recounted on the postcards but this visit in no way detracted from the main purpose of the visit, to report his findings to the company.

From 1908 there had been leisurely visits to Berlin. Wernher produced letters of introduction for the Colonial Secretary, Dern Bury, to tour South West Africa. In return they received little but promise of co-operation. In Kimberley the De Beers Diamond Committee deliberated on proposals for the Diamanten-Regie-Gesellschaft (the Regie) to act as a major extension of company in April 1913. This company had been set up in 1906 by the German administration of South West Africa to prevent overproduction and price crashes. All diamonds had to be sold through this organisation which became a state-run monopoly. Francis Oats agreed to a joint tender with the syndicate, as in line with purchases made of smaller mines (Voorspoed and Kaffefontein) to stop their production possession of the South West diamond fields, would prevent them undercutting De Beers prices.

The inspection party arrived early in 1914 and made a thorough examination of conditions of production and prospects for cooperation. Another initiative for agreement with Germany came from an unexpected quarter in South Africa. Because the forecast of failing yields from the Premier Mine and therefore lower revenue, the Transvaal Government held 60% of shares, Jan Smuts, in his capacity as Minister of Finance, met company directors in 1913 December to approve a plan to bring the South West mines into a producers cartel.

The German Foreign Office approved the initiative. Thus as war approached there was a surprising willingness to co-operate in one sector of the mineral market. The boards of De Beers, Premier, Taggersfontein and Kaffefontein met in Johannesburg for the first time as a Union's producers delegation, though they did not agree on a

De Beer's White Train; Dorothy Oats (nee Brown)
with Francis Edwin in 1912.

joint strategy. Once in London their representatives joined with Meyer Gerhard for the Regie and the four members of the Syndicate to hammer out terms for an international quota. The agreement was signed on 31st July. War broke out only a few days after the conference rose and the agreement was never put into force. The diamond beach of South West Africa was seized almost immediately by South African troops and eventually all of the German diamond operations found themselves part of Oppenheimer's Consolidated Diamond Mines.

In the De Beers Annual General Meeting later this year, only Francis Oats dared voice the hope that the agreement might, some day, be renewed "when the Union Government will take the place of the German Government". With the invasion of South West Africa by South Africans already under way, this statement was warmly applauded.

CHAPTER 13
THE LAST YEARS

"And time flows fast away" (JFL)

War, illness and death, 1914 -1918

The War came close to most people. Francis Oats with his directors had to arrange to shut down the mines; the production was nil and men were paid off but quotes from the Annual General Meetings will show some of the policies and concerns of the company during these years and these reports with earlier ones of the doings in Parliament showed also where Francis Oats was and what he was about.

Outlining the happenings in these last years of his life are copies of quite a few personal letters between members of his family so that this side of his life comes much more to the fore. Details of how the war affected them, the partings and would they meet again. Two of his sons were for some of the war with the Expeditionary Forces in South East Africa. The German Colony there and the struggles to oust them were a very different kettle of fish to the swift overthrow of the enemy and the over-running of their colony in South West Africa at the beginning of hostilities. In the east every step of the way was painfully contested, with the extremely capable commander, General Von Lettow, in charge of the German forces.

There are letters between the sons and their father, some to their sister, the odd cable, letters from England from Dorothy to her husband Freathy and visa versa. Also communications from Francis Oats to his solicitor and to his sons when they returned to the United Kingdom. An intimate picture can be built up of Francis showing another side from the formal one of the company reports or the speeches. It is often noticeable how tender and concerned he could be even in business affairs.

Francis crossed the seas to Britain in 1915 and again in the following year. German raiders were off the coasts of South Africa and submarines menaced the English shores near the approaches to the ports of the United Kingdom. His wife, Elizabeth Ann accompanied him home in 1916. Probably she had been in Port Elizabeth or Kimberley at the outbreak of war. Back in St. Just she went to live once more in Carne House which was more convenient for her in several ways. The carriage horses were commandeered long before and Dorothy's horse Peggy had earlier still gone to war with Freathy. Elizabeth Ann, was not very mobile but, at least, in the centre of town her friends and relatives could easily visit her and the Chapel was not far from this house. Another reason for residing here was that this year, Dorothy, her daughter-in-law, had gone up with the three little sons to live in a rented cottage in Surrey nearer her parents.

Porthledden had been quite a worry for Dorothy for staff had left for the forces and nanny and nursemaid too, to do war work. The farm was under-staffed and at

Francis with Rolls Royce on a bridge. This is probably in South Africa as the advertisement is for "Challenge" brand Magaliesberg tobacco.

one time when there was a lack of a dairymaid she suggested that she should do this work. Apparently she was not very well as mentioned in a letter from her father-in-law to the solicitor in charge of his affairs in Cornwall. Thus it was arranged that for the time Porthledden should be left with a skeleton staff.

As mentioned, all three of Francis' sons were in the forces, all belonging to the Territorials. Freathy, by now a major, and Giles were in the same battalion, part of the 134 (Cornwall) Heavy Brigade, Royal Artillery, based for a time at Tregantle Fort, across the Tamar from Plymouth. Later they served in the East African campaign. Freathy went out in 1915 returning in 1917 to Woolwich and then to the Somme. Giles was in Africa 1915-16 and then back to Britain to be trained in siege warfare and posted to Gallipoli.

From a Cornish newspaper was this report, "Captain Frank Oats has two sons fighting in East Africa and the third son Wilfred, a doctor, suffering from trench fever and other complications induced by the mud and water of Flanders. He had resigned his Territorial commission in order to get to the fighting line".

28th December 1915
Twenty Seventh Annual General Meeting
Chairman Presiding. Mr. Francis Oats

Rebellion
These are events of the past, pray God they may never recur. We in South Africa, thanks to a strong Union Government, who were loyal to the Imperial Government, and to the King, have dealt with the difficulties as they have arisen. The cloud that was threatening in the West has been removed, but

there is still the menace in East Africa; there also, South Africans will, we hope, prove as loyal and true and efficient as in the South-West, and we trust after this to suffer no danger to this country from any incursion of Germans.

Then the Chairman quoted from a speech by Sir David Harris in which "he referred to the charge that this Company, or its Directors, were essentially German", and which it will be well to embody in my speech today. Sir David said, "He would first give the composition of the De Beers Board. There were twelve Britishers, one Frenchman....and there were three naturalised Germans. These later were, Sir Carl Meyer and his son was in the British army; Mr. Breitmeyer, who had a son in the British army, and Mr. Hirschhorn (a bachelor). Followed by a list of men, sons of directors, fighting and some who had died fighting". Mr. Oats goes on in his speech to mention, "news since then of the death in action of the son of an old Kimberley resident and one time Director of this Company, Mr. Isodore Dreyfus. Also his brother-in-law, Mr. Bernheim, who had acted as alternative for some time as a director, his only son too, has just been killed, both these young men were killed in the month of October last, fighting the Germans in France. That statement is, I think, a sufficient answer to the charge that the Directors are essentially German. It seems to me incredible to think that anyone can speak of Directors of this Company as being German in any sense of the word, or of sympathising with the Germans. I would say more: I don't think anyone can serve the German cause so much, and so well – or so badly – as those who attribute to those trying to do their best in British interest, disloyalty to those British interests. I wish we could put our foot on that snake. It is the manifestation of that spirit which assists the Germans as much as anything else....We should all be careful not to ascribe to others disloyalty – a too common practise – unless that disloyalty is very well known and very plainly shown".

In May 1915 Francis Oats landed in Plymouth. His son Freathy writing to his wife at Porthledden from the Royal Hotel in Plymouth, writes:-

A few lines to let you know the Pater got back alright. We all three went off in a tug this morning to meet him and found him looking fairly well but a little pale. It was a tiresome job getting off the boat and through the customs lasting till mid-day. Now Pater has gone off to Town and as far as I could gather his programme is to stay there till the weekend after next, when he intends going down to St. Just. I am applying for leave to go to Town immediately, partly to call at the War Office and partly to do some work with the Pater....I am also asking for leave to come home when Pater gets down....

Another communication of the same sort, this time the letter is headed from the Langham Hotel, London, Sunday June 8th.

Pater and I are going down to Bletchingley for lunch, and I go back to Plymouth either by afternoon or night train.

82

Drawing of Francis Oats, nicknamed "Kimberley", in the
South Africa magazine of 7 February 1914

August 8th he wrote again to his wife at Porthledden, from Plymouth.

> Well, the Pater is well on his way out by this time, and I hope clear of the
> submarines. Poor old Pater, he did not want to go much this time....

August 29th, he writes again this time from Charlton Camp, Woolwich.

> Thank you for your letter with Pater's letter to me. I'm glad they got through
> to Madeira without any great excitement....

(These letters speak for themselves, "the three" in the first letter were the sons of
Francis Oats, and the mention of 'Bletchingley' to lunch was to his wife's parental
home).

One presumes Francis Oats was in St. Just at Porthledden as he planned and that
some time during this stay Freathy got leave to come home. In December Freathy
with his battalion sailed in a troop ship for South Africa.

From letters from Freathy to Dorothy in England it can be deduced that Francis
Oats was back in Britain in 1916.

From Freathy to Dorothy February 14th East African Expeditionary Force:

> Now I'll stop, sweetheart and say adieu for the time, please give my love to
> the Pater and Mater.

On February 22nd another was written, extracts below:-

> Yes, by all means keep the car until the Pater comes back, when Hilda perhaps
> will be able to get down to Porthledden and drive him about". He also adds
> that his father "will not stay at Porthledden if there is not enough work for
> him to do"!

The matter of the car is quite interesting, I am doubtful if Hilda, Dorothy's sister,
could come down, she was about to volunteer to join the Royal Automobile Corps,
but to get about St. Just and further afield to the various mines was not easy any
longer with the shortage both of petrol and men to drive.

As I have mentioned previously, between my mother and her father-in-law there
was understanding and deep affection. Before the end of his stay in England she had
moved up to a rented house in a neighbouring village to her parents. However, she
travelled down from Surrey to bid Francis goodbye and safe voyage. There had been
for a short while some idea of her accompanying him out to South Africa, and of
course her husband was out there still, but nothing came of it. Francis Oats was keen
but she had responsibilities towards her children and the seas were not safe.

When she came down to bid grandfather farewell, she brought her son Jack (John
Freathy) with her, and at Penzance took a taxi out to St. Just (my own feeling is she
came unannounced, to surprise and please him and would have stayed overnight at

Carne House with Elizabeth Ann; as mentioned, Porthledden was only cared for by a skeleton staff).

Below I quote from Jack's own memories.

> I only saw him once. I remember arriving and the big doors swing open and sudden bright lights and going through the inner doors saw several men sitting at an enormous table, and the figure from the far head of the table coming to this inner door to embrace mother. Warmth of welcome and the bright lights fixed a photographic memory for me.

Jack was two and a half years old then, being born in February 1914. A lively remembrance which he kept clear in his mind all his life and which he told me about towards the end of his own life.

The last letter for 1916 that I have is from Freathy, then serving with 134 (Cornwall) Heavy Brigade, Royal Artillery, African Expeditionary Force, to his father now back in situ, written from East Africa,.

He thanks his Father for his kindness in ordering dried fruits from the De Beers farms to be sent up to East Africa for his men; he also mentions cigarettes having arrived as well as for the battery, sent by his sister Elise. His brother Giles, he writes, had apparently got over his touch of fever and was to have rejoined soon but has had a relapse and is, he believed, being sent to a convalescent home in the Usambaro Hills somewhere near Mombu or Karagwe. He gives something of the conditions there at Morogoro whilst they wait for the shattered railway line to be repaired (blown up by the retreating Germans) and ending this letter, "You should get this letter somewhere about your birthday, 29th October and I hope by the time the next one come comes round, you will be able to have it and many others in peace. Your loving son, Freathy."

In the first few months of 1917 Francis Oats travelled widely looking after various De Beers concerns as far afield as Dundee in Natal and to Somerset West in the Cape. Freathy, writing to his wife, said he had wished to write on 1st January but had been unable to do so as they had been in action but writing on March 6th, this time from Cape Town where he was sent to finish convalescing after malaria, "On arrival at Cape Town the Pater met the boat and I saw him for about half an hour. He is looking fairly well generally but is getting older all the time and he is very shaky on his legs, and has great difficulty walking about".

Francis wished to make a journey this year too, back to Britain but his fellow directors were against it and persuaded him to defer it; they knew he was ill and of course that the voyage was very dangerous. In a later letter to his wife, Freathy writes:-

> I'm leaving here today to go with the Pater to Kimberley and to the collieries in Natal. My original intention was to have gone down here to Port Elizabeth last Thursday. But the Pater is anxious about the collieries and wants to go at once. There is no reason why I should go and I'd really prefer to go down to Elise and get in some rest, but I think the Pater wants my company a bit. Now

Pater is calling me to breakfast, so adieu.

How long the two were gone I am not sure, nor where they parted, but think it could have been Bloemfontein, as in a letter Francis mentions this town. He would have gone on to Kimberley and Freathy to Durban for soon he is writing to his Father to tell him he had been to a sugar factory called Campbell. He also mentions his cousin Rundle Olds who had just been to an asbestos factory. The latter was manager of the Cape Asbestos Mine in Namaqualand.

There continued the flow of correspondence between Freathy and his father who wrote to him on May 29th, probably addressing it to the Garrison in Cape Town. Whether Freathy managed any leave left to him at his sister's home in Port Elizabeth is not recorded. My mother did not keep all the letters perhaps, or some of the transports were torpedoed and the mail lost. Freathy had been sent at the end of his leave to take temporary command of the King George Fort, Cape Town, whilst the regular commander was on leave or elsewhere.

This letter of May 29th throws light on Francis Oats' state of health and also on his continuous interest in the farm at Cape Cornwall which was run by a bailiff. He tells his son, "I have been very ill for ten days but I am now much better. I suppose this confounded cold weather has aggravated it a good deal, but I hope by the end of June I shall be able to go down to Port Elizabeth for a month or more to take the Zwartkop Water".

He encloses a letter he wishes posted on to his solicitor, Grylls, in Cornwall which is to do with the running of the farm Nanpean. "Read it first and add any comments or suggestions yourself and post it....".

From this letter it is clear the running of the farm in war time is proving very difficult. Sufficient here to mention it as it shows the wide interests Francis had in no way shrugged off because of distance or war for by then he was really a sick man.

The last point of interest in this letter is his mention of his daughter-in-law Dorothy and being "a little concerned about her". "For I fear she is not well and probably this business is worrying her; I would be very sorry for it to do that because she has three children, her husband is away, and she has not been well for a long time. I hope you will try to keep all the troubles you can off her shoulders".

In May this year he was invited to lay the foundation stone for the new Wesleyan Methodist Sunday School in Bean Street. When he and Elizabeth Ann first came together to Kimberley they lived in West Side near the mine and they attended the nearby Chapel. Later after moving to their home in Belgravia district it was to the Bean Street Chapel they went to services (and where I found my way one Sunday in 1990). In 1994 in a newspaper advertisement the Chapel was up for sale and I believe the little Sunday School was burnt down).

In June came a cable from Freathy to him from Cape Town bidding him goodbye and on June 8th writing to his wife Dorothy, he tells her he has orders to board a troopship sailing shortly.

Francis Oats remained as busy as ever in spite of failing health. Writing to Freathy he tells him "I returned here a few days ago from a visit to the Cape Asbestos

Silver trowel presented to Francis for laying the foundation stone
for the Bean Street Methodist Sunday School, Kimberley 23 May 1917

Company mine. I went via Uppington and came back over the De Beers farms....as
to asbestos, our people in London must do something to use the short asbestos with
cement for purposes of making slate for roofing".

In October his daughter, Elise Leith sent him a telegram, "Should like to visit you
for a while. Could I travel up Thursday morning? When are you going to Montague?
Love."

So this month for a little while he had the care and comfort of his daughter near
him and in the following month he went to Cape Town to take the waters of the spa

at Montague, hoping to relieve his condition. Whilst he was there a cable came for him from his son Giles sent from Alexandria. This was November 22nd, and sent on from Kimberley by the secretary, E. F. Raynham to c/o Ligdyn.

However Francis Oats was back in Kimberley before the end of this month for on 30th he chaired the AGM. This was to be for him the last time and a sad year's close. From the Chair he had to announce the news that the company had lost four directors that year and the last one was his old friend and associate, Sir Starr Jamieson. His varied career now ended.

CHAPTER 14
THE END

1918

"And time which none can bind leaves love behind"

F rancis Oats belongs to the past, to the powerful company he served so faithfully, to the Cape, to diamonds, to Cornwall, to tin, but at the last he belongs to his family. So he will simply be grandfather here in his last days and during his struggle with ill health. It was his strength and energy that kept him in life, so now the habit of work forced him to try to stay in harness almost to the end.

Early in the year grandfather returned to the Montague Spa for further treatment. He had found relief there in October and November the previous year but this time there was no marked improvement. He was suffering from a paralysing and enfeebling disease of the central nervous system and throughout the year he became progressively worse. He returned to Kimberley by February 20th, travelling back once more through the Rhodes fruit farms which always gave him much pleasure. And one remembers how only recently he had been arranging for the dried fruits from these orchards to be sent up to the troops.

Later this year comes a lengthy letter from Freathy at Forge Cottage, Oxted where the family had a rented cottage. He writes,

> "I was very glad to get your letter of April 25th, even though this is not written by you, as it is such a long time since I had a letter from you. I wish you could have some good man with you to look after you and be a confidential clerk as well. You don't know how this would ease our minds at home. Since I last wrote you I have had one day and a weekend in Cornwall, and I will try to give you some account as to how I found things".

He proceeds to give grandfather an up-to-date account of Wheal Basset, Levant Mine, Bissoe and Porthledden Mine, with the arrangements for new heating for the house. It gives grandfather immediate news of his wife at Carne House with her companion; of how some of Cornwall's mines fared, of a son at the front; of another son and family. One is glad in a roundabout way that grandfather's two sons had served in East Africa for at least he had contact with them during some part of the war years – with sight and comfort from them these last years, but his wish to travel to Britain in 1917 was unfulfilled.

Back in Kimberley Francis did have the services of a trained male nurse, arranged for him by the company. He must always have been reassured to know that in the same land and not too far away lived his daughter, her doctor husband and their children. As we shall see he had no wish to leave Kimberley or his work and worried about all he should be doing.

In August after correspondence between the directors, Dr.. Leith and Elise, the latter two came up to Kimberley to persuade grandfather to go back with them. This he was reluctant to do, but on August 7th he did consent to travel to Port Elizabeth with them, and they journeyed there in the De Beers rail coach.

Mr. Hirschhorn, a director, and a friend of long-standing, corresponded with the family and it was in a letter to him from Robert Leith that the details of grandfather's last illness are revealed, and of the three weeks he was in Bird Street, the Leith's home. In 1990 when I re-met my cousin Jean Leith at her Walmer home in Port Elizabeth she told me she could remember grandfather 'shuffling' about in her home. She was born in 1913.

1, Bird Street,
Port Elizabeth,
17th August, 1918.

Dear Mr. Hirschhorn,

You will by now have reached Kimberley and have heard all news there is of Mr. Oats and also that Mr. Westcott called and told me of your cable to Freathy Oats and of all other kindnesses on behalf of Mr. Oats. You have also doubtless seen Ashe [a doctor] who would give you details of the nature of Mr. Oats' illness and of the outlook.

We had a comfortable journey down here thanks largely to the thoughtfulness and generosity of the Directors in placing De Beer's car at Mr. Oats' disposal. My wife and I both appreciate this very much and I hope you will tell the other Directors how much we feel indebted to them.

The patient was rather silent and I think a little depressed at the outset of the journey but since his arrival has been better. He is mentally clearer since he came down and physically stronger too I think. He spends most of the day out of bed, talks about all general topics and dictates letters, mostly about home and family affairs. For the most part his mind is clear though at times his memory becomes hazy and he confuses ideas. Now that he feels better, it is more difficult to reconcile him to the life of inactivity down here. He speaks daily of returning to Kimberley "tomorrow".

Today he insisted on going out to Zwartkop for a bath and though one wished him to remain quiet on account of his helpless condition, we had to let him go as he was so insistent. If he improves further, I fear we shall have difficulty in inducing him to lead a quiet life. He has made all sorts of plans about visiting Koegas, Swaziland, and after the war, Cornwall, Turin and other places.

As regards the real nature of the trouble and his prospects, I expect you have got the facts from Ashe. The improvement since he came down here one regards as only temporary. The trouble is actually a degeneration of the central nervous system starting in the spinal cord and slowly spreading to the brain and higher centres. He may have periods of apparent improvement or where the trouble may appear stationary for a time; but the general tendency will be for the disease to become worse until he becomes physically helpless and unable to leave his bed and the mind also to become less active and finally a blank. How long this may last no one can say. The downward course may be rapid and if he should develop any complication such as pneumonia, diarrhoea, etc., he could not stand it for long. On the other hand he may yet go on for many months.

At present the main difficulty is keeping him content when he wants to do so many things that he is unable to do yet feels he can and wants to. I do not think he is in the condition to transact any important business matters and if the necessity arises we shall avail ourselves of your kindness in offering to attend to them for him.

I hope you are well and with kind regards,

I am,

Yours sincerely,

(Signed) R. M. LEITH

Mercifully the disease worked rapidly, as grandfather was to die within a few weeks of his arrival in Bird Street. Below is the telegram Elise sent to the Secretary of De Beers, Mr. Raynham, at Kimberley.

"Papa passed away peacefully without regaining consciousness ... 2.15 ... this afternoon. Funeral tomorrow at 3 o'clock. No flowers."

So grandfather died on Sunday September 1st and on another Sunday September 1st was born a great-granddaughter, Jennifer Frances in 1946.

"And the threads are woven daily in and out"

The Funeral - September 2nd

Only family and some very close friends attended the quiet internment but there was to be one exception. The head scoutmaster sent a wire from Kimberley requesting that Scouts might be present at the burial. "This was because Mr. Oats had been a real friend to the movement and was President of the Kimberley Scout Association".

Grandfather would have been really touched by such a wish and accordingly scouts were indeed present upon that September afternoon and the Last Post was sounded by the Assistant Scout Master of the Port Elizabeth troop, the patrol being made up of one member from each of the eight patrols. Also present was Sir Edgar Walton, President of the Scout Association in this city.

Over his grave now lies a slab of unpolished grey/blue granite to which the stonemason affixed a shield-shaped stone to carry the raised lettering with his name.

IN MEMORY OF
FRANCIS OATS MINING ENGINEER
OF
ST JUST-IN-PENWITH CORNWALL
AND
KIMBERLEY
BORN AT GOLANT 29TH OCTOBER 1848
DIED AT PORT ELIZABETH
1ST SEPTEMBER 1918

Adieu mon chére grandpére. The story is almost ended.

Below is De Beers farewell to Francis Oats from the chair, taken at the 1918 Annual General Meeting by Colonel Sir David Harris. The two had known each other from the early days in Kimberley and must have discussed many problems together and had good times in each others company. Colonel Harris and Mr. Hirschhorn seem the two within the company that grandfather had most constantly near him, Colonel Harris supporting him at such meetings and, in his failing days, Mr. Hirschhorn kindly helping behind the scenes.

Col. Harris said from the Chair:-

"At the last Annual Meeting the Chairman referred in sympathetic and touching terms to the death of four Directors of this Company, and the loss thus sustained by the removal of gentlemen who had been long and honourably associated with us in the conduct of its affairs. Today it is my sad duty to mention yet another great loss in the death of Mr. Francis Oats, who was a Director of this Company for 28 years and occupied the responsible position of Chairman since 1908. Mr. Oats was a self-made man who overcame the disadvantages he laboured under in early life and by dint of hard study, indomitable persistency and determination, laid the foundations of the distinguished and remarkable career which came to an honourable close in his 70th year. His devotion to this Company was unbounded and his solicitude for the welfare of its employees was uppermost in his thoughts. His whole soul was wrapped up in De Beers Company and his activities on its behalf knew no limitations, though even then he found time to take an active interest in the affairs of South Africa generally and to render valuable services in many ways. On behalf of the Board, I express our deep regret at the loss of a capable and indefatigable colleague. (Hear, Hear).

The grave in Port Elizabeth.

The family had many letters and telegrams of condolence but I will quote only two here.

The telegram from General Louis Botha, Prime Minister of South Africa:

> "Have just heard of the death of Francis Oats and would be obliged if you would convey to the bereaved relatives....an expression of my deepest sympathy with them... Not only has this Country lost a man of outstanding ability and force, but I have suffered the loss of a friend for whom I have

always entertained the warmest feelings of respect and admiration".

And from Oscar Satchel, Headmaster of Kimberley School:

> "Regrets, etc.. Mr. Oats was keenly interested in all the youth of the Diamond Fields and gave many practical proofs of his earnest desire to promote everything which tended to improve conduct, character and education in scholars.
>
> Personally I wish to express my own deep regret. He was, I know, interested in my acceptance of the appointment as Headmaster and I feel sorry that he was never physically able to visit the school after I took up my appointment."

Grandfather's will was detailed but straightforward. Because the three sons were all in England a power of attorney was arranged and the two executors were his son-in-law, Dr. Robert Leith and the director and friend, Mr. Hirschhorn, their attorneys were Messrs. Haarhoft, Hertog and Lange who arranged all in the usual manner, dates for the collection and payment of debts, the will and accounts on view in the Assistant Master's Office for three weeks.

Plaque on the boarding school at Kimberley.

There were set out the very last purchases made by grandfather before he left Kimberley always the most poignant reminders of a person, the dozen handkerchiefs, two rug straps, two picture frames and payment to the newsagent. The final public remembering was in 1920 when his old friend, Colonel Harris, opened a new building at the boarding house of Kimberley School, naming the building "Francis Oats House". "It is for me a happy way to say farewell", he said.

In South Africa boys had to travel long distances to attend school. At first they were boarded privately. This boarding house had long been planned and De Beers had again financed something to help education, or the children who would be educated there. Whilst in the city in 1990, I peeped inside and in the dining hall everything was neatly laid and ready for another meal. In the hallway hung a photograph of grandfather, a different one from the one I have been accustomed to. This one is full face, more genial it seemed, perhaps enjoying a throng of youngsters close by! Altogether this is a fitting way to have his name commemorated. Here in an establishment to teach tomorrow's leaders and workers for South Africa, what better example to youth. This man with his passion for education, starting in his own boyhood, who took all that was available and used it to its uttermost.

"On the broad bosom of the stream of time the little thoughts and concepts of man froth and bubble and have their day. Some of these bubbles travel further than others, bearing with them, memories of those who sent them forth so bravely floating long ago. Then they too break upon the rock of change, and vanish like the rest into thin air."

An extract from "Cornwall and its People" published 1932 by Hamilton-Jenkin.

APPENDICES

Family Trees

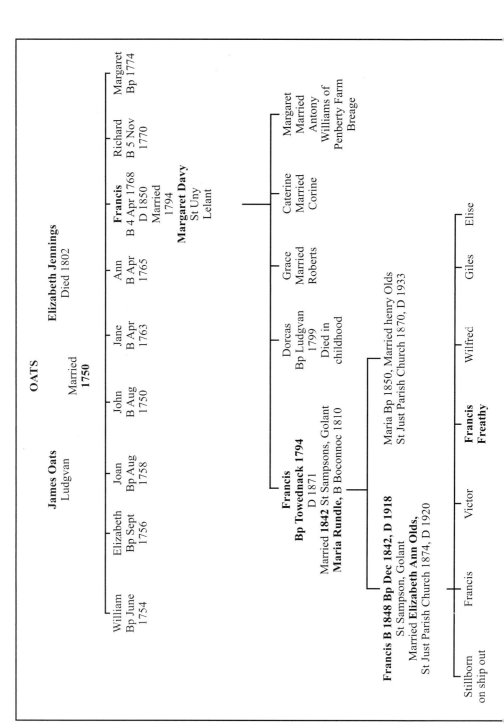

OATS

James Oats
Ludgvan

Married **1750**

Elizabeth Jennings
Died 1802

William
Bp June
1754

Elizabeth
Bp Sept
1756

Joan
Bp Aug
1758

John
B Aug
1750

Jane
B Apr
1763

Ann
B Apr
1765

Francis
B 4 Apr 1768
D 1850
Married
1794
Margaret Davy
St Uny Lelant

Richard
B 5 Nov
1770

Margaret
Bp 1774

Dorcas
Bp Ludgvan
1799
Died in
childhood

Grace
Married
Roberts

Caterine
Married
Corine

Margaret
Married
Antony
Williams of
Penberty Farm
Breage

Francis
Bp Towednack 1794
D 1871

Married **1842** St Sampsons, Golant
Maria Rundle, B Boconnoc 1810

Maria Bp 1850, Married henry Olds
St Just Parish Church 1870, D 1933

Francis B 1848 Bp Dec 1842, D 1918
St Sampson, Golant
Married **Elizabeth Ann Olds,**
St Just Parish Church 1874, D 1920

Stillborn
on ship out

Francis

Victor

Wilfred

Francis
Freathy

Giles

Elise

The families
RUNDLE and FRETHY

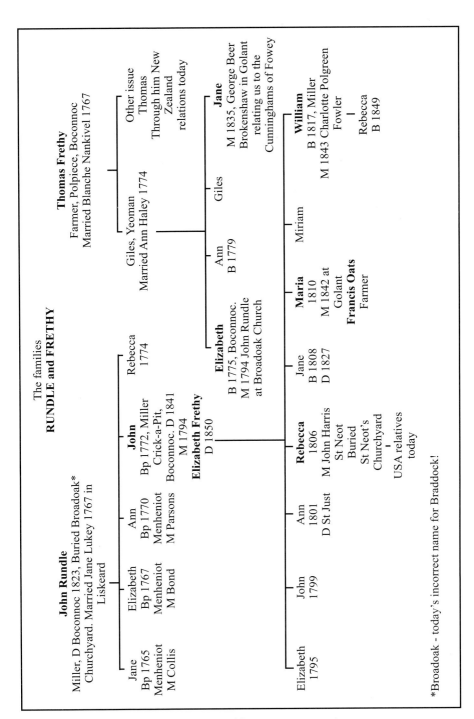

John Rundle
Miller, D Boconnoc 1823, Buried Broadoak*
Churchyard. Married Jane Lukey 1767 in
Liskeard

Thomas Frethy
Farmer, Polpiece, Boconnoc
Married Blanche Nankivel 1767

Jane
Bp 1765
Menheniot
M Collis

Elizabeth
Bp 1767
Menheniot
M Bond

Ann
Bp 1770
Menheniot
M Parsons

John
Bp 1772, Miller
Crick-a-Pit,
Boconnoc. D 1841
M 1794
Elizabeth Frethy
D 1850

Rebecca
1774

Giles, Yeoman
Married Ann Haley 1774

Other issue
Thomas
Through him New
Zealand
relations today

Elizabeth
B 1775, Boconnoc.
M 1794 John Rundle
at Broadoak Church

Ann
B 1779

Giles

Jane
M 1835, George Beer
Brokenshaw in Golant
relating us to the
Cunninghams of Fowey

Elizabeth
1795

John
1799

Ann
1801
D St Just

Rebecca
1806
M John Harris
St Neot
Buried
St Neot's
Churchyard
-
USA relatives
today

Jane
B 1808
D 1827

Maria
1810
M 1842 at
Golant
Francis Oats
Farmer

Miriam

William
B 1817, Miller
M 1843 Charlotte Polgreen
Fowler
|
Rebecca
B 1849

*Broadoak - today's incorrect name for Braddock!

99

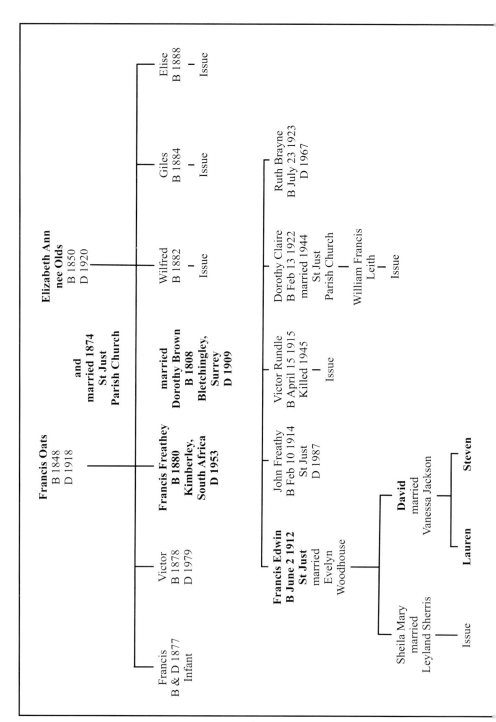

Francis Oats
B 1848
D 1918

and married 1874 St Just Parish Church

Elizabeth Ann nee Olds
B 1850
D 1920

Francis
B & D 1877
Infant

Victor
B 1878
D 1979

Francis Freathey
B 1880
Kimberley,
South Africa
D 1953

married
Dorothy Brown
B 1808
Bletchingley,
Surrey
D 1909

Wilfred
B 1882
–
Issue

Giles
B 1884
–
Issue

Elise
B 1888
–
Issue

Francis Edwin
B June 2 1912
St Just
married
Evelyn
Woodhouse

John Freathy
B Feb 10 1914
St Just
D 1987

Victor Rundle
B April 15 1915
Killed 1945
–
Issue

Dorothy Claire
B Feb 13 1922
married 1944
St Just
Parish Church

William Francis
Leith
–
Issue

Ruth Brayne
B July 23 1923
D 1967

Sheila Mary
married
Leyland Sherris

Issue

David
married
Vanessa Jackson

Lauren

Steven

INDEX

101